This book is from

the kitchen library of

_____

_____

Mr. Food®
EASY TEX-MEX

ART GINSBURG
Mr. Food®

WILLIAM MORROW AND COMPANY, INC.

NEW YORK

Library of Congress Cataloging-in-Publication Data

Ginsburg, Art.
    Mr. Food® easy Tex-Mex / Art Ginsburg.
        p.   cm.
    Includes index.
    ISBN 0-688-14578-7
    1. Cookery, American—Southwestern style.   2. Mexican American cookery.   3. Quick and easy cookery.   I. Title.
TX715.2.S69G55   1997
641.5979—dc21   96-47462
                                                                             CIP

Printed in the United States of America

First Edition

1 2 3 4 5 6 7 8 9 10

BOOK DESIGN BY MICHAEL MENDELSOHN OF MM DESIGN 2000 INC.

Dedicated to
all the varied cultures that have
come together to create the
lively food tastes that we know as

TEX-MEX

ACKNOWLEDGMENTS

Boy, did I ever have a fun time writing this book! Well, that was mainly due to the spicy team that made it all happen.

First I have to thank the people who continue to help turn my ideas into reality: Howard Rosenthal and Caryl Ginsburg Fantel. You two are as good as gold!

And where would I be without my dynamite kitchen staff?! Patty Rosenthal, Janice Bruce, Cheryl Gerber, and Jo Ann Skelton, thank you for all the testing, tasting, and retesting you've done with me. And thanks also to Laura Ratcliff for working your magic on the wording of each recipe, and Joe Peppi for overseeing every aspect of the recipes from start to finish.

Of course, my family and staff are always close by, willing to offer the services of their taste buds! All I can say to Ethel, Steve, Chuck, Carol, Tom, Chet, Marilyn, Beth, Helayne, and Alice is: Thanks for never taking a siesta when I needed your opinions and help. . . no matter how large a lunch we had to have!

Now what would Tex-Mex cooking be without a little zing? I certainly get all the zing I need from the gang at William Morrow, under the guidance of Al Marchioni and my editor, Zachary Schisgal. Zach, you always seems to be able to smooth out any bumps we encounter along the way, while keeping us moving on our hectic schedules! And I know you get a lot of support from the expertise of Richard Aquan, Deborah Weiss Geline, Carrie Weinberg, Michael Murphy, Jackie Deval, and Anne Cole.

 v i i

ACKNOWLEDGMENTS

Of course, no list of thanks would be complete without my expression of appreciation to my book agent, Bill Adler, to my extremely creative book designer, Michael Mendelsohn, and to my illustrator, Philip Scheuer. I tip my *sombrero* to all of you for another job well done!

Of course I've got a big "*Gracias!*" to my readers and viewers, and also to the following companies and organizations for helping to make all of my recipes zestier, tastier, and full of "OOH IT'S SO GOOD!!®"

California Avocado Commission
Dr. Randi Cohen
Land O' Lakes, Inc.
McIlhenny Company, makers of Tabasco® Pepper Sauce
Old El Paso/Pillsbury
Pace Foods
Sandcastles Property Design & Development,
    Fort Lauderdale, Florida
Sargento Cheese Company Inc.
Who-Song & Larry's Restaurant & Cantina,
    Fort Lauderdale, Florida

CONTENTS

INTRODUCTION

I know you know me as Mr. Food, but my staff has taken to calling me *Señor* Food! Actually, I don't blame them. You could say that I've been bitten by the bug . . . the Tex-Mex bug! I used to be one of those people who'd eat my fill of tacos and fajitas once in a while, but since I discovered the wide variety of Tex-Mex foods, I can't stop. And I want to share my excitement with you.

Are you one of the many people who think that all Tex-Mex foods are spicy? Well, that's not so! As you look through these recipes, you're going to be amazed not only by how easy they are, but also by their diversity of tastes. And you'll be thrilled to realize that you've already got most of the ingredients in your pantry and fridge, or they're easy to pick up at your local supermarket. I mean, I've seen too many Tex-Mex recipes with long lists of ingredients, most of which I can't even pronounce, let alone find without going to a bunch of different specialty stores or buying from catalogs.

For each of these recipes, I've done a lot of testing and refining to make sure I've come up with the easiest, tastiest version possible. And when it comes to adjusting the "heat" of each one, you'll find loads of options in Pick a Pepper (page xviii), which shows some of the most popular peppers used in today's Tex-Mex cooking. You may or may not choose to give these a try, but I wanted to show you how to add a little Wow! to your dishes. And before you do that, be sure to read Pepper Safety on page xxi because not only can these little guys burn your taste buds, but they can burn your skin and eyes, too. Be careful, please!

So, what's in this book besides tacos and burritos? Well, just wait until you see my easy homemade salsas and sauces. They're kind of like the hot fudge part of an ice cream sundae, and there's a whole chapter of them! There's fresh-from-the-garden-tasting Pico de Gallo (page 5) and colorful Confetti Salsa (page 6). I've included my family's favorite Fast Guacamole (page 10) and others like my cross-cultural Fiesta Marinara Sauce (page 13) and Texas Barbecue Sauce (page 12) that'll liven up any meal. Now don't get nervous. . . . If you'd rather use bottled salsas, that's fine. I just like you to have options!

If you've eaten in a trendy restaurant lately, then you've probably seen some of the tasty Mexican-inspired appetizers that are popular now. I've got a whole chapter of those, too. Whether you set out to dip or nibble, you're in for a treat with Southwestern Black Bean Dip (page 17), Queso Dip (page 20), Spicy Beef Empanadas (page 27), and Nachos Grande (page 25). They're all guaranteed crowd-pleasers.

Okay, so you're in the mood for something a little lighter. Turn to my Soups and Salads. Whether you choose Tortilla Soup (page 37), Zingy Gazpacho (page 42)—one of my all-time favorites— or Piñata Soup (page 38), you'll be sure to serve a soup with a real burst of flavor. It's the same with the salads, from Mexican Caesar Salad (page 43) to Taco Salad (page 45), and even Ranch Potato Salad (page 48). And because I love salad dressings so much, I've even included a few snappy ones that'll add a whole new thrill to your own favorite salads. Nope, there's nothing ho-hum here!

Tex-Mex for brunch?! Why not? The classic Huevos Rancheros (page 58), plus Mexican Toast (page 63) and Breakfast Burritos (page 57), offer a perfect way to wake up your taste buds. Cheesy Spoon Bread (page 66), Border Biscuit Bake (page 60), and the

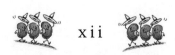

INTRODUCTION

other fritters, breads, and baked items I've included here fit in just right at any time of day!

Yes, we have tortillas! As a matter of fact, you're going to be amazed at all the possible rolling, wrapping, and folding combinations I've got for you to try. At the beginning of the tortilla chapter (page 71), I've got info on all the different types of dishes you can make with tortillas. Want to sink your teeth into a nice beefy burrito? Or maybe you'd prefer a taco? Or a tostada or enchilada? They're all here, not to mention chimichangas and easy recipes for making your own flour and corn tortillas (pages 89 and 90). And, if you're really adventurous, try making empanadas with Homemade Empanada Dough (page 91). They're certainly worth a little extra effort!

When we think of Tex-Mex, we think "hearty." So that's where my meat chapter comes in. Maybe your gang's in the mood for Mexican Pot Roast (page 95). Or maybe you'd rather serve up bowls of Range Chili (page 102), Ropa Vieja (page 101), or a nice rich stew. There are plenty to choose from! And hearty also means ribs slathered with flavorful sauces, burgers, chops, and steaks with tastes unique to the Southwest. They're in here, too!

Even though I love meat, don't think I've forgotten about good old chicken and turkey. Uh-uh! I've developed some incredible finger-licking recipes. Of course, you'll need to use a fork or spoon if you're going to serve up a batch of Saucy White Chili (page 124) or Mojo Chicken (page 120). And I highly recommend the tender and flavorful Margarita Chicken (page 119); no, you don't drink it with a straw!

Fish and seafood are popular in Tex-Mex cooking, too. Whether you fancy Gulf of Mexico Shrimp Scampi (page 137), Galveston Bay Swordfish (page 131), or Chilled Salmon with Avocado Salsa (page 133), you're in for a "reel" treat!

Now you're going to need some go-alongs . . . you know, the side dishes that make ordinary meals extraordinary. There are beans in so many colors and combinations, and rice, potatoes, even yuca. You're going to have quite a time deciding whether to make Golden Fried Plantains (page 152), Southwestern Vegetable Medley (page 148), or any of the others. Good luck!

The choices don't stop there! It's even tough deciding what to drink! Should it be Frozen Virgin Margaritas (page 157) or a Tequila Sunrise (page 163)? Those are just two of the possibilities that are here, along with Mexican Coffee (page 166) and a good old Coffee Milk Shake (page 164) that's so thick and satisfying it could be a dessert.

Well, I said that magic word: dessert, so I might as well remind you to save room for it, since it's going to be almost impossible to resist my Lime Margarita Bars (page 169), Texas Sticky Buns (page 186), and Adobe Bars (page 170). They make great snacks, too. And for adding the perfect finishing touch to a special dinner, you've just got to serve Chocolate Tres Leches (page 181) or Spanish Flan (page 182).

Okay, get going! You've gotta start your cooking so that
your taste buds will be buzzing and your belly will be full.
Then you can sit back and enjoy a siesta
while dreaming of all the
"OOH IT'S SO GOOD!!®"

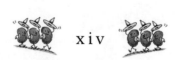

xiv

TOPPINGS BAR

The great thing about doing a book on Tex-Mex foods is that the combinations of ingredients are endless. And putting the same things together in a different way can practically create a totally different meal. Although most of the recipes in this book call for specific toppings, many can be easily changed according to your own likes or dislikes. My philosophy has always been for you to make things to your own tastes, so here's a list of toppings that can be used to create your own toppings bar for tacos or fajitas, or for topping virtually anything (except desserts and drinks, of course!) in this book.

Use just one or two toppings, or put them all out for a *grande* buffet! Go ahead—have a ball!

Avocados—Select fresh avocados that are ripe yet not mushy. Remove the pit, peel, and thinly slice (see the illustrations below and instructions on p. xvi) or cut into chunks.

TOPPINGS BAR

1. Halve avocado lengthwise, cutting around the seed.
2. Tap the seed carefully with the edge of a sharp knife. Twist and lift out the seed.
3. Peel back the skin and cut the avocado as desired. Sprinkle with lemon juice to preserve the color.

Black (ripe) olives—Slice or chop them yourself, or buy them already cut up. Drain well before using.

Cheese—Oh, the choices! Shred or grate your favorites, or buy already-shredded cheese . . . it's so convenient! My Tex-Mex favorites are Monterey Jack, Colby, and Cheddar. The selections are super. Also look for Mexican cheese blends—some are even preseasoned. And whether you're starting with a block of cheese or shredded cheese, if you prefer a little extra zing, try using the ones studded with jalapeño peppers.

Chopped green chilies—Available whole or chopped in cans or jars, these are usually mild-flavored.

Cilantro—An herb that looks like flat leaf (Italian) parsley, cilantro should be rinsed and then shaken to remove excess water. Coarsely chop and lay it on a cookie sheet to dry slightly before sprinkling over finished dishes as a fresh, flavorful garnish.

Guacamole—Make your own (page 10) or buy it prepared, fresh or frozen. It's available in both traditional and spicy styles, so be sure to read the labels and get what you want!

Iceberg lettuce—Wash and drain well. Cut the head in half, then into very thin slices, almost shredding it. That's it!

Jalapeño peppers—Available fresh, canned, or bottled, sometimes pickled and whole, sliced, or chopped. Cut fresh jalapeños into rings. Use any type of jalapeño sparingly to spice up your Tex-Mex dishes. Please refer to my sections Pick a Pepper (page xviii) and Pepper Safety (page xxi).

Picante sauce—A thinner version of salsa that is generally not chunky in texture.

TOPPINGS BAR

Salsa—Traditional salsa is a combination of chopped tomatoes, onions, chilies, and garlic. Our markets have a large variety of salsas—fresh, bottled, and canned—with a choice of textures and preparations from traditional to chunky and cooked. And the ingredients vary with the addition of other vegetables. There are even selections of fruit salsas available, too, in a range from mellow and sweet to fiery hot.

Sour cream—I recommend using a brand with a thick consistency because it'll hold up better than looser ones. Experiment with different brands to find the right one. Sure, light or reduced-fat versions are fine if you prefer, but whichever one you choose, be sure to stir it up well just before serving.

Taco sauce—A hot red sauce that's not as spicy as hot pepper sauce and is especially good for spooning over tacos, burritos, and other Tex-Mex dishes.

Tomatoes—Choose firm, ripe red tomatoes and keep them at room temperature until ready to use. Then rinse and dry, cut in half, and, if you prefer, gently squeeze out the seeds. Coarsely chop, slice, or cut into chunks, depending on how you're going to use them.

Additional sauces and salsas, including enchilada sauce, green salsa, even fruit salsas, are widely available and offer even more taste variety. Choose any salsa or sauce in the first chapter to add extra zing to your finished recipes.

PICK A PEPPER

Have you ever walked into a supermarket and seen a bunch of unusual-looking peppers at the produce counter? Most likely, many of them are chili peppers. There are so many pepper varieties available to us today that it's hard to keep them all straight! And because of cross-pollination, there are new types of peppers still popping up.

That's why I've put together an easy guide showing and describing the most popular ones. This should help you recognize some of the varieties in your local stores.

Since most chili peppers are native to Mexico, you'll find many different types of them in Tex-Mex recipes. Still, many are hard to find without going to specialty shops. That's why I've limited my use of fresh chilies in the recipes here—I've tried to stick with the most common types. Of course, if you've got a favorite type that you'd like to add to any of these dishes, go ahead. Just do it in small amounts, 'cause a little goes a long way—and you can always add more!

Ancho chilies are dried poblano chilies. Deep reddish-brown in color, they're the most popular dried chilies. Mildly hot in flavor, anchos can often be replaced by chili powder or crushed red pepper.

Bell peppers are certainly a staple on our produce counters. Very mild and sweet, bell peppers are traditionally found in green and red varieties, although today they're also readily available in yellow, orange, and deep purple.

California/green chilies are very popular on the West Coast (hence, the name). Ranging in intensity from mild to hot, they're usually found canned.

Cayenne pepper is hot stuff! It's ground from dried hot peppers. Actually, I should say from *very* hot peppers, so use it sparingly!

Chili powder was originally just finely ground dried chilies. Today's chili powder is really a blend of spices, including ground cumin, garlic and onion powders, and oregano. Of course, the blend differs from brand to brand, with some much hotter than others.

Crushed red pepper is used frequently in Italian foods; it's the spice we often see on dinner tables in Italian restaurants. Very hot, it should be used sparingly. It's made by flaking dried peppers, including their hot seeds.

Hot pepper sauce is a combination of the pulp of hot chilies, vinegar, and salt. A dash or two goes a long way and the strength varies greatly by brand. Available in supermarkets, most hot pepper sauces indicate their intensity right on the label.

Jalapeño peppers are 2 to $2^1/2$ inches in length and are best when bright green in color. Jalapeños are the most popular chili peppers and can be found fresh in the produce section of most supermarkets. They're usually hot, although some are on the mild side. You can also find them canned or bottled, sometimes pickled in the international section of the supermarket.

Pasilla chilies are similar to ancho chilies, but thinner and longer, with a slightly hotter flavor.

Pimientos are from the pepper family, too. Very mild in taste, they're bright red and are found canned or jarred in the pickle section of the supermarket.

Poblano chilies are mild-flavored and similar in size and shape to a green bell pepper. They are the most frequently used chilies in authentic Mexican cooking and are found canned in some specialty shops, but are not commonly available throughout the United States. Green bell peppers can be substituted for these.

Serrano chilies are small and green to bright red in color. They grow to about $1^{1}/_{2}$ inches in length. They're very hot! Jalapeño peppers can be used in place of these.

PEPPER SAFETY

Please be careful when handling fresh chili peppers, because chilies contain oils that can burn your eyes and skin, not just your taste buds. You'll be fine if you follow a few basic rules:

- Hot peppers should *not* come in contact with the skin and eyes, so I recommend wearing plastic or rubber gloves when working with them. If those aren't available, you can protect your hands by coating them with a layer of vegetable oil. But this will also make your hands slippery, so you'll have to be extra careful when handling a knife.

- When working with hot peppers, never wipe your eyes with your hands!

- You can also burn your tongue and mouth if you get adventurous and taste even a bit of a hot chili. So, when you do try one, do so with just an ever-so-small piece at first to determine how hot it really is (the intensity will vary). Then add a little at a time to whatever you're making. (You can always make a dish hotter later on by adding a few dashes of hot pepper sauce or more chopped chilies.)

- Whether you use gloves or coat your hands with oil, always wash your hands and nails thoroughly with soap and water after working with chilies.

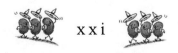

SOME LIKE IT HOT, SOME NOT

Before you roll up your sleeves and start cooking, let me share a little something with you: In the recipes that include salsa or picante sauce as an ingredient, I didn't specify hot, medium, or mild. That's because I want you to select just how spicy each recipe will be. Also, the "temperature" or heat intensity of these prepared products will vary from brand to brand. Sample a few brands and intensities and choose whichever you prefer for your various uses. Remember, after you make a recipe, you can always add a few dashes of hot pepper sauce, or a little more cayenne pepper—even some chopped fresh chilies. I'm giving you the starting points from which you're going to create your own recipes. No one knows your gang like you. So cook up a storm at whatever temperature you prefer!

A NOTE ABOUT PACKAGED FOODS

Packaged food sizes may vary by brand. Generally, the sizes indicated in these recipes are average sizes. If you can't find the exact package size listed in the ingredients, whatever package is closest in size will usually do the trick.

I always encourage using your own favorite brands, but be aware that, when making the recipes in this book, using different brands of products, especially salsa and spices, will probably alter the taste of a recipe. Some companies tend to make their products on either the mild or the spicy side, so you may want to experiment with one or two different product brands. And remember, you can always add a little more spice or "heat" (see page xxii), so have a ball!

SAUCES AND MORE
SALSAS Y MÁS

1

HOMEMADE SALSA

ABOUT 4 CUPS

Some say salsa is the basis of good Mexican-style cooking. Well, sure it is! We dip into it, top with it . . . we even cook with it! See—basics are important. You've gotta give this a shot.

2 cans (28 ounces each) whole
   tomatoes, chopped and drained
1 large onion, finely chopped
½ a medium-sized green bell
   pepper, finely chopped

½ teaspoon minced garlic
1 teaspoon lemon juice
3 fresh jalapeño peppers,
   stems and seeds removed,
   finely chopped

Combine all the ingredients in a large bowl; mix well. Cover and chill for at least 1 hour to allow the flavors to "marry" before serving.

NOTE: You can make this as mild or hot as you want. For a hotter salsa, add 1 or 2 more chopped jalapeño peppers.

SALSA VERDE

ABOUT 2 CUPS

In Spanish, *salsa verde* means "green sauce," but to me, it means even more variety for my Mexican feasts.

¾ pound fresh tomatillos, husks removed and quartered (about 2 cups)
¼ cup chopped red onion
1 tablespoon minced fresh cilantro

1 fresh jalapeño pepper, stem and seeds removed, chopped
¾ teaspoon salt

In a food processor that has been fitted with its steel cutting blade, combine all the ingredients and process until well chopped, but not puréed. Serve immediately, or place in an airtight container and chill until ready to use. Lasts for up to 1 week in the refrigerator.

NOTE: If fresh tomatillos are unavailable, you can substitute 2 medium-sized green tomatoes and 1 teaspoon lime juice.

PICO DE GALLO

ABOUT 3 CUPS

Talk about "fresh tasting" and "versatile"... you'll think this great sauce was just picked fresh from the garden.

2 medium-sized ripe tomatoes, finely chopped

½ a medium-sized onion, finely chopped

3 fresh jalapeño peppers, stems and seeds removed, finely chopped

1 tablespoon chopped fresh cilantro

¼ teaspoon salt

Juice of ½ a lime

Combine all the ingredients in a large bowl; mix well. Cover and chill for at least 1 hour, or until ready to serve.

NOTE: This makes a great dip and also a zesty topping for tacos and fajitas. And remember, make it milder or more intense by adjusting the amount of jalapeños.

CONFETTI SALSA

ABOUT 4 CUPS

Not only will you need those sunglasses for the bright Mexican sun, you'll also need 'em when you serve up a batch of this colorful change-of-pace salsa.

1 can (15¼ ounces) whole kernel corn, rinsed and drained
1 can (15 ounces) black beans, rinsed and drained
1 jar (7 ounces) roasted red peppers, drained and chopped

1 jar (16 ounces) salsa
2 tablespoons chopped fresh cilantro
3 scallions, chopped

Combine all the ingredients in a medium-sized bowl; mix well. Cover and chill for at least 2 hours, or until ready to serve.

NOTE: For more heat, add 2 or 3 seeded and chopped fresh jalapeño peppers.

RED CHILI SAUCE

ABOUT 2 CUPS

Make a double batch, 'cause this will last for weeks in your refrigerator if you cover it tightly (if it isn't gobbled up sooner, that is)!

1 can (10¾ ounces) tomato purée
1 medium-sized onion, cut into
   quarters
1 garlic clove

1 tablespoon vegetable oil
2 tablespoons chili powder
1 teaspoon sugar
1 teaspoon salt

In a blender or a food processor that has been fitted with its steel cutting blade, combine all the ingredients; blend until smooth. Pour into a small saucepan and cook over low heat for 8 to 10 minutes, stirring occasionally, or until the sauce is slightly thickened.

NOTE: This is a great sauce for enchiladas and if you keep some on hand, you can use it instead of the enchilada sauce in El Paso Enchiladas (page 85), or as a taco or fajita topping.

TWO-GRAPE SALSA

ABOUT 1½ CUPS

"Two-grape or not two-grape?" If that is the question, I say, "Why not?" It tastes good and it's really refreshing!

¾ cup chopped seedless green grapes
¾ cup chopped seedless red grapes
½ a medium-sized red bell pepper, chopped
1 scallion, chopped

1 tablespoon chopped fresh cilantro
1 tablespoon olive oil
1 tablespoon lime juice
1 fresh jalapeño pepper, stem and seeds removed, finely chopped

Combine all the ingredients in a medium-sized bowl; mix well. Cover and chill for at least 1 hour, or until ready to serve.

NOTE: Serve with tortilla chips or even as a fruity side dish to add fresh color and flavor to your dinner.

MANGO SALSA 1-2-3

ABOUT 2½ CUPS

Living in South Florida gives me the luxury of being able to pick mangoes from a tree right in my own backyard. I wanted something to do with these besides eating them by themselves, so I made this Mango Salsa . . . and now we can all make it easy as 1–2–3!

1 ripe mango, pitted, peeled, and finely chopped
½ a medium-sized green bell pepper, finely chopped
½ a medium-sized red onion, finely chopped

2 tablespoons orange juice
2 teaspoons lime juice
⅛ teaspoon salt
¼ teaspoon black pepper

Combine all the ingredients in a large bowl; mix well. Cover and chill for at least 2 hours, or until ready to serve.

NOTE: This salsa makes a perfect topping for grilled fish or chicken, and it even makes a nice side dish alternative.

FAST GUACAMOLE

ABOUT 1⅓ CUPS

You can make this so fast, you'll wonder why you ever bought ready-made guacamole. Just make sure the avocados are ripe. And if they do need a little extra ripening, just place them in a brown paper bag in a warm place until you're ready to go.

2 ripe avocados, pitted and peeled
1 tablespoon lime juice
2 tablespoons picante sauce

¼ teaspoon garlic powder
¼ teaspoon salt

Combine all the ingredients in a large bowl. Use a fork or potato masher to blend well. Serve immediately.

NOTE: The best avocados for guacamole are the Hass avocados, which are small and dark green, almost black. If you want to make this in advance, go ahead. But after you make it, place the avocado pit on top of the guacamole, cover, and chill until ready to use. The pit will help reduce the darkening of the guacamole and help maintain its bright green color. Bet you didn't know that!

MOCK-A-MOLE

ABOUT 3 CUPS

According to the dictionary, mock means "imitation" or "simulation." And since this looks and tastes so much like guacamole, I make it when I don't have any ripe fresh avocados on hand ('cause I've always got canned peas in my cupboard). Well, to me, as long as it tastes good, it works!

2 cans (15 ounces each) peas, rinsed and drained
½ cup sour cream
3 scallions, chopped
3 fresh jalapeños, stems and seeds removed

2 tablespoons lime juice
2 garlic cloves
½ teaspoon ground cumin
½ teaspoon salt

In a food processor that has been fitted with its steel cutting blade, combine all the ingredients and process until well blended. Serve immediately, or store in an airtight container in the refrigerator until ready to serve. Lasts for up to 3 days in the refrigerator.

TEXAS BARBECUE SAUCE

ABOUT 3 CUPS

Real Texans always make their own barbecue sauce, and now, so can you. No, no, you don't need a cowboy hat or a Texas accent—all the accent is on taste.

2 cups water
2 cups ketchup
½ cup firmly packed dark brown
   sugar
½ a medium-sized onion, chopped

2 tablespoons prepared yellow
   mustard
2 teaspoons hot pepper sauce
2 teaspoons Worcestershire sauce

In a large saucepan, combine all the ingredients and bring to a boil over high heat, stirring frequently. Reduce the heat to medium-low and cook, stirring frequently, for 30 to 40 minutes, or until the sauce is thick and glossy.

NOTE: This sauce is great with Cowboy Ribs (page 100), or you can use it in just about any recipe that calls for barbecue sauce.

FIESTA MARINARA SAUCE

ABOUT 4 CUPS

Yes, sirree . . . this is one of my favorite examples of cross-cultural cooking. I love the full, fresh flavor of Italian red sauce combined with the zest of Mexican red sauces.

1 can (10¾ ounces) tomato purée
3 large ripe tomatoes, chopped
1 large sweet onion, chopped
1 large green bell pepper, chopped
1 fresh jalapeño pepper, stem and seeds removed, chopped

1 tablespoon chopped fresh cilantro
¼ cup chili powder
¼ teaspoon cayenne pepper
½ teaspoon salt

Combine all the ingredients in a large saucepan; mix well. Bring to a boil over high heat, then reduce the heat to medium-low and simmer for 20 minutes. Serve immediately.

NOTE: Serve over pasta and top with shredded Monterey Jack cheese for a real south of the border pasta fiesta.

TACO SEASONING

ABOUT ½ CUP

Why not make your own taco seasoning with five spices you have right in your cupboard? You'll always have it on hand, and for a lot less money than store-bought mixes.

¼ cup chili powder

4 teaspoons paprika

4 teaspoons dried oregano

2 teaspoons ground cumin

2 teaspoons salt

Place all the ingredients in a small airtight plastic container. Close tightly and shake until thoroughly combined.

NOTE: Use as much as you like to season your recipes with homemade Tex-Mex zip. A quarter cup of this seasoning can be substituted for a 1¼-ounce envelope of dry taco seasoning mix in your homemade tacos, or in any recipe that calls for taco seasoning. Try it for seasoning steaks and roasts, too!

APPETIZERS/
APERITIVOS

SOUTHWESTERN BLACK BEAN DIP

ABOUT 3 CUPS

Roll up your sleeves, get out the tortilla chips, and you're ready for some good Southwestern dippin'.

2 tablespoons olive oil
2 tablespoons all-purpose flour
2 cans (15 ounces each) black
   beans, rinsed and drained
1 can (14½ ounces) ready-to-use
   beef broth

2 tablespoons chili powder
1 garlic clove, minced
¼ teaspoon dried oregano
⅛ teaspoon ground cumin
½ cup (2 ounces) shredded
   Monterey Jack cheese

In a medium-sized saucepan, heat the oil over medium heat. Add the flour and cook for 2 to 3 minutes, until the flour has browned, stirring frequently. Add the remaining ingredients except the cheese; mix well. Cook for 5 to 6 minutes, until well blended and bubbling, stirring often. Reduce the heat to low and simmer for 25 to 30 minutes, or until slightly thickened. Pour into a serving bowl and top with the cheese; serve warm.

NOTE: You can make this ahead of time, without adding the cheese. Just cover and store it in the refrigerator for up to 3 days. Just before serving, rewarm it, then top with the cheese.

FRESH AVOCADO DIP

ABOUT 2 CUPS

You can dip tortilla chips for a Mexican flair, or try dipping fresh-cut veggies for that fresh-from-the-garden taste. Or what about good old saltine crackers? We've always got those on hand for any-time snacking.

3 ripe avocados, pitted and peeled
1 garlic clove, chopped
½ cup salsa
2 teaspoons lemon juice
¼ cup chopped fresh cilantro or
   4 teaspoons dried cilantro

½ teaspoon salt
¼ teaspoon black pepper
1 medium-sized ripe tomato,
   chopped

Place all the ingredients except the tomato in a medium-sized bowl; mash with a potato masher or fork until chunky. Stir gently until well combined. Pour into a 9-inch pie plate or shallow serving bowl and top with the chopped tomato.

NOTE: Don't worry if you can't find ripe avocados. You can always place firm ones in a paper bag and keep in a warm spot in your kitchen for a day or two before you plan to make this. That should do the trick!

SIX-LAYER DIP

8 TO 10 SERVINGS

A winner every time, this one's got lots of tasty layers without taking lots of work!

1 can (16 ounces) refried beans
1 container (8 ounces) prepared guacamole (see Note)
1 container (16 ounces) sour cream
1 package (1¼ ounces) dry taco seasoning mix

2 cups (8 ounces) shredded Mexican cheese blend
1 medium-sized ripe tomato, chopped
4 scallions, thinly sliced

Spread the refried beans on a 12-inch round serving platter, then spread the guacamole over the beans. In a medium-sized bowl, combine the sour cream and taco seasoning; mix well, then spread over the guacamole. Sprinkle with the cheese, then the tomato, then the scallions. Serve immediately, or cover and chill until ready to serve.

NOTE: To make your own guacamole in no time, see Fast Guacamole, page 10.

QUESO DIP

ABOUT 3 CUPS

In Mexico, practically everything is made *con queso* (with cheese). So what could be more authentic, satisfying, and simple than this cheese dip?

1 cup salsa
1 can (4 ounces) chopped green
    chilies, drained

4 cups (16 ounces) shredded
    Cheddar cheese

In a medium-sized saucepan, combine all the ingredients and cook over medium-low heat for 8 to 10 minutes, or until the cheese is melted and smooth, stirring frequently. Serve immediately.

NOTE: This dip is a natural with tortilla chips or as a great taco topper.

MEXICAN CHEESE DIP

ABOUT 2 CUPS

Here's another cheesy dip that's sure to please. In Mexico, it's called *queso fundido*, but I call it one of my favorites!

½ pound hot Italian turkey
   sausage, casing removed

1 pound Mexican-flavored
   processed cheese spread,
   cut into cubes

In a medium-sized skillet, cook the sausage for 8 to 10 minutes over medium heat, or until browned, crumbling it as it cooks. Drain off the excess liquid and reduce the heat to medium-low. Add the cheese cubes and cook for 5 to 7 minutes, or until the cheese melts, stirring constantly. Serve immediately.

NOTE: One, two ingredients—it couldn't be easier! You can serve this as a dip or use it as a filling for quesadillas. For each quesadilla, just spread this between 2 flour tortillas and cook in ½ teaspoon oil in a large skillet for 3 to 4 minutes, turning halfway through the cooking.

MEXICAN SPOONER

10 TO 14 SERVINGS

I call this a "spooner" because it's like a pie that you get to spoon onto your favorite tortilla chips.

1 can (16 ounces) refried beans
1 cup salsa
1 can (4¼ ounces) chopped black olives
1 can (4 ounces) chopped green chilies, drained

1 medium-sized ripe tomato, chopped
1 cup (4 ounces) shredded Cheddar cheese
½ cup sour cream
1 scallion, thinly sliced

Preheat the oven to 350°F. Spoon the beans into the bottom of a 9-inch pie plate that has been coated with nonstick vegetable spray. Spread over the bottom and up the sides to form a "crust." Layer with the salsa, olives, chilies, and tomato, then top with the cheese. Bake for 30 minutes, or until heated through. Remove from the oven, dollop with the sour cream, and top with the sliced scallion. Serve warm.

NOTE: Sometimes I like to top this with fresh jalapeño peppers sliced into rings instead of the scallion.

JALAPEÑO POPPERS

ABOUT 2 DOZEN

Trendy restaurants are offering cheese-stuffed jalapeño peppers as an appetizer. Well, you can make your kitchen just as trendy when you make these yourself.

12 medium-sized fresh jalapeño peppers
1 package (8 ounces) cream cheese, softened
1 cup grated Parmesan cheese
1 cup all-purpose flour, divided
½ cup cornmeal, divided
¾ cup milk
½ teaspoon salt
½ teaspoon black pepper
Vegetable oil for deep-frying

Split the peppers in half lengthwise, cutting through the stems, then remove the seeds (see Illustration 1). In a small bowl, combine the cream cheese and Parmesan cheese. Firmly press a heaping teaspoonful of the cheese mixture into each pepper half (see Illustration 2). Cover and chill for at least 2 hours. In a medium-

Split 'em in two!

Fill 'em with the cheese!

sized bowl, combine ½ cup flour, ¼ cup cornmeal, the milk, salt, and black pepper. In another medium-sized bowl, combine the remaining ½ cup flour and ¼ cup cornmeal. Dip the stuffed pepper halves into the milk mixture, then into the dry mixture, coating thoroughly with each. Fill a large saucepan or soup pot with 2 inches of vegetable oil and heat over medium-high heat until hot but not smoking. Carefully fry a few peppers at a time for 2 to 3 minutes, or until golden brown. Drain on paper towels and serve immediately.

NOTE: See my tips on handling hot peppers on page xxi.

NACHOS GRANDE

6 TO 8 SERVINGS

This is so big, you'd better save it till you have a hungry crowd on your hands.

1 package (8 ounces) tortilla chips
1 pound ground beef
1 package (1¼ ounces) dry taco seasoning mix
1 can (16 ounces) refried beans
2 cups (8 ounces) shredded Mexican cheese blend
1 can (2¼ ounces) sliced black olives, drained

1 can (4 ounces) chopped green chilies, drained
¾ cup salsa
½ cup sour cream
1 scallion, thinly sliced
2 tablespoons chopped fresh cilantro

Preheat the oven to 400°F. Place the tortilla chips in a mound on a 12-inch pizza pan and set aside. In a large skillet, brown the ground beef over medium-high heat for 7 to 10 minutes, or until no pink remains, crumbling it as it cooks. Stir in the taco seasoning and refried beans. Cook for 3 to 5 minutes, or until thoroughly heated. Spoon over the tortilla chips, then top with the shredded cheese, olives, and chilies. Bake for 7 to 9 minutes, or until the cheese is melted. Remove from the oven and top with the salsa, sour cream, scallion, and cilantro. Serve immediately.

NOTE: Since you know what your gang likes, feel free to omit any of these toppings or add any favorites.

BAKED CHEESE DROPS

ABOUT 2 DOZEN

Cheese, salsa, and beer all rolled into one. . . . This is my kind of food for "drop"-in company!

1 cup biscuit baking mix
½ cup (2 ounces) shredded
 Monterey Jack–pepper cheese

¼ cup salsa
⅓ cup beer

Preheat the oven to 450°F. Combine all the ingredients in a medium-sized bowl; mix well. Drop by heaping teaspoonfuls 2 to 3 inches apart onto a rimmed baking sheet that has been coated with nonstick vegetable spray and bake for 8 to 10 minutes, or until golden. Remove from the oven and serve immediately.

NOTE: Serve with some additional warmed salsa for dipping.

SPICY BEEF EMPANADAS

16 EMPANADAS

We might know these simply as turnovers brimming with meat. The actual Mexican name is *empanada*, and when you make them, boy, will your gang be impressed!

1 pound ground beef
1 cup salsa
½ teaspoon salt

¼ teaspoon black pepper
2 packages (15 ounces each) folded refrigerated pie crust

Preheat the oven to 375°F. In a large skillet, brown the ground beef for 5 to 7 minutes over medium-high heat, or until no pink remains, crumbling the beef as it cooks. Add the salsa, salt, and pepper; mix well. Remove from the heat and let cool slightly. Unfold the pie crusts and cut each of the 4 crusts into 4 circles, each 4 inches in diameter. Spoon 2 heaping tablespoonfuls of the meat mixture into the center of each piece of dough and fold in half, forming half-moons. Seal the edges firmly with your fingers, then crimp the edges with the tines of a fork. Place on a baking sheet that has been coated with nonstick vegetable spray and bake for 20 to 22 minutes, or until golden brown. Serve immediately.

NOTE: When you have the time (and the desire), you can make Homemade Empanada Dough (page 91).

JALAPEÑO CHEESE TURNOVERS

ABOUT 18 TURNOVERS

If you like fried wontons, crispy egg rolls, or crunchy knishes, you're gonna love the crisp you get in every bite of these. . . .

1 package (8 ounces) cream cheese
1 fresh jalapeño pepper, stem and seeds removed, chopped
¼ cup grated Parmesan cheese
1 package (6 ounces) wonton wrappers, thawed if frozen
Nonstick vegetable spray

Preheat the oven to 450°F. In a medium-sized bowl, combine the cream cheese, jalapeño, and Parmesan cheese; mix well. Place 1 wonton wrapper on a work surface. Dip your fingers in a small bowl of water and moisten the edges of the wonton. Place 1 tablespoon of the cheese mixture in the center of the wrapper and fold diagonally to form a triangle. Seal the edges firmly with your fingers. Place the turnover on a 10" × 15" baking sheet that has been coated with nonstick vegetable spray. Continue with the remaining cheese mixture and wonton wrappers. Spray the tops of the turnovers lightly with nonstick vegetable spray and bake for 6 to 7 minutes, or until golden and the edges are crispy. Serve immediately.

NOTE: Serve these with some warm jalapeño jelly—it's perfect as a dipping sauce. Why, you can even make your own with the recipe on page 68! Oh, while you're filling the turnovers, be sure to keep the unfilled wonton wrappers covered with a damp paper towel so they won't dry out. Then wrap any remaining wonton wrappers in plastic wrap and reserve for future use.

CANTINA PIZZA

4 TO 6 SERVINGS

Like the warming rays of the sun, this will warm the hearts and stomachs of your *familia* (your family).

One 12-inch prepared pizza shell
1 can (14½ ounces) Mexican-
    style stewed tomatoes, drained
2 cups (8 ounces) shredded
    Mexican cheese blend

1 package (3 ounces) cooked
    chorizo sausage, cut lengthwise
    into thin slices

Preheat the oven to 425°F. Place the pizza shell on a pizza pan and spread the tomatoes evenly over the top. Sprinkle with the cheese, then lay the slices of chorizo over the cheese. Bake for 8 to 10 minutes, or until the cheese is melted and the crust is crisp and brown.

NOTE: Add some fresh chopped jalapeño pepper to the stewed tomatoes for an extra bit of spiciness.

BLACK GOLD SNACK MIX

ABOUT 12 CUPS

Finding a bowl of this snack mix in your family room is almost as good as finding oil in your backyard . . . so make sure to always have some of this on hand. (Okay, I'll admit it—this *is* really good, but I'd rather find oil!)

3 cups oven-toasted corn or rice
   cereal
2 cups corn chips
1 cup unsalted mini pretzels
2 cups mini cheese sandwich
   crackers
1 cup fish-shaped cheese crackers
1 can (10 ounces) unsalted
   mixed nuts

1 cup shelled pumpkin or
   sunflower seeds
½ cup (1 stick) butter
¼ cup cayenne pepper sauce
2 tablespoons Worcestershire
   sauce
2 tablespoons dry chili
   seasoning mix

Preheat the oven to 250°F. In a large bowl, combine the cereal, corn chips, pretzels, crackers, nuts, and seeds; set aside. In a medium-sized saucepan, heat the remaining ingredients over medium heat for 3 to 4 minutes, or until the butter melts, stirring frequently. Pour over the snack mix and toss to coat well. Spread onto 2 large rimmed baking sheets and bake for 1 hour, stirring occasionally. Remove from the oven and allow to cool slightly. Serve warm, or let cool completely, then place in an airtight container and keep sealed at room temperature.

NOTE: Some toasted corn and rice cereals are a combination of both flavors, so it's okay to use one of those types, or even use half corn and half rice cereals.

TEXAS CAVIAR

6 TO 8 SERVINGS

Hold on, pardner! There are no fish eggs here. Texans have a different idea of what most of us think of as caviar. (And in my book, it's just as tasty . . . but in a whole new way!)

2 cans (15 ounces each) black-eyed peas, rinsed and drained
½ a medium-sized onion, finely chopped
1 tablespoon chopped fresh cilantro

1 medium-sized tomato, finely chopped and drained
1 fresh jalapeño pepper, stem and seeds removed, coarsely chopped
½ cup bottled Italian dressing

In a large bowl, combine all the ingredients except the dressing. Pour the dressing over the top and toss to coat well. Cover and chill for at least 2 hours, or until ready to serve.

NOTE: Serve with tortilla chips for dipping or use as a filling for a quick cold vegetable burrito.

YOUR OWN POTATO SKINS

12 POTATO HALVES

These can definitely be your own potato skins, 'cause after you cook the potatoes, you get to fill them your own way.

6 baking potatoes
½ cup vegetable oil
1 teaspoon salt

1 teaspoon onion powder
1½ teaspoons chili powder

Preheat the oven to 400°F. Scrub the potatoes and pierce the skins with a fork. Bake for 45 to 60 minutes (or microwave on high power for 12 to 15 minutes), until fork-tender. Let the potatoes cool slightly, then cut each potato in half lengthwise and hollow out each half with a spoon, leaving a shell about ¼ inch thick. Save the potato pulp for another use. In a medium-sized bowl, combine the remaining ingredients. Rub the potato skins, inside and out, with the oil mixture and place on a 10" × 15" rimmed baking sheet. Bake for 40 to 45 minutes, or until the edges are crispy and brown. Add your favorite toppings, or see the next pages for suggestions.

JALAPEÑO CHEESE TOPPING
ENOUGH TOPPING FOR 12 POTATO SKINS

2 cups (8 ounces) shredded
  Mexican cheese blend

2 tablespoons chopped fresh
  jalapeño peppers

Preheat the oven to 400°F. Top prepared baked potato skins evenly with the cheese and jalapeño peppers, then bake for 3 to 4 minutes, or until the cheese melts. Serve immediately.

PIZZA TOPPING
ENOUGH TOPPING FOR 12 POTATO SKINS

1 jar (16 ounces) salsa
2 cups (8 ounces) shredded
  Monterey Jack cheese

1 package (3 ounces) cooked
  chorizo sausage, chopped

Preheat the oven to 400°F. Spoon the salsa evenly into prepared baked potato skins, then sprinkle with the cheese. Top with the chorizo sausage and bake for 3 to 4 minutes, or until the cheese melts. Serve immediately.

CHILI CON CARNE TOPPING
ENOUGH TOPPING FOR 12 POTATO SKINS

1 can (15 ounces) chili con carne
  with beans
2 cups (8 ounces) shredded
  Mexican cheese blend

½ cup sour cream
2 scallions, thinly sliced

Preheat the oven to 400°F. In a small saucepan, warm the chili over medium heat. Spoon the chili into prepared baked potato skins. Sprinkle with the cheese and bake for 3 to 4 minutes, or until the cheese melts. Remove from the oven and dollop with the sour cream. Top with the sliced scallions. Serve immediately.

SOUR CREAM AND GUACAMOLE TOPPING
ENOUGH TOPPING FOR 12 POTATO SKINS

1 container (16 ounces) sour
  cream
1 container (8 ounces) prepared
  guacamole

1 can (2¼ ounces) sliced black
  olives, drained

Spoon the sour cream evenly into prepared baked potato skins. Spoon the guacamole over the sour cream and sprinkle the sliced olives over the top. Serve immediately.

SOUPS AND SALADS/
SOPAS Y ENSALADAS

TORTILLA SOUP

5 TO 6 SERVINGS

Tortilla soup is to Mexico what chicken soup is to the United States. Now, I don't know if it helps cure colds, but it sure satisfies appetites!

1 can (14½ ounces) ready-to-use
   chicken broth
1 can (14½ ounces) ready-to-use
   beef broth
1 medium-sized onion, finely
   chopped
1 cup salsa

½ teaspoon ground cumin
2 tablespoons vegetable oil
4 corn tortillas, cut into
   ⅛" × 3" strips
1 cup (4 ounces) shredded
   Monterey Jack cheese

In a large saucepan, combine the broths, the onion, salsa, and cumin over medium heat. Bring to a boil, then cover and reduce the heat to low. Simmer for 20 minutes. Meanwhile, in a medium-sized skillet, heat the oil over medium heat. Sauté the tortilla strips for 2 to 3 minutes, or until lightly browned, turning to brown both sides; drain on paper towels. When ready to serve, ladle the soup into serving bowls and top evenly with the tortilla strips and cheese. Serve immediately.

NOTE: For a heartier soup, add leftover cooked shredded, cubed, or chunked chicken along with the broths.

PIÑATA SOUP

6 TO 8 SERVINGS

As colorful as a Mexican piñata, and bursting with flavor, spoonful after spoonful.

½ pound ground beef
1 medium-sized onion, chopped
1 can (14½ ounces) diced
    tomatoes, undrained
1½ cups water
1 can (16 ounces) kidney beans,
    undrained

1 can (8 ounces) whole kernel
    corn, drained
1 can (8 ounces) tomato sauce
1 teaspoon chili powder

In a soup pot, brown the ground beef and onion over medium heat for 5 to 7 minutes. Add the remaining ingredients; mix thoroughly. Reduce the heat to low and simmer, uncovered, for 30 minutes, or until thoroughly heated.

NOTE: Tortilla Crisps (page 87) make a great go-along.

TEXAS STEAK SOUP

8 TO 10 SERVINGS

Texans are known for liking everything big, including their steaks. That's why I like to cut the steak into large slices for this soup—to give it hearty Texas body.

2 tablespoons vegetable oil

1½ pounds boneless beef sirloin steak (½ inch thick), trimmed and cut into 1½" × ¼" strips

1 large sweet onion, chopped

4 cups water

3 large potatoes, washed and cut into ½-inch cubes

3 large carrots, cut into ¼-inch slices

2 beef bouillon cubes

1 teaspoon ground cumin

½ teaspoon black pepper

In a soup pot, heat the oil over medium-high heat and brown the steak strips. Add the onion and cook for 6 to 7 minutes, or until the onion is tender. Add the remaining ingredients and bring to a boil; cover and reduce the heat to low. Simmer for 40 to 45 minutes, or until the potatoes and carrots are tender.

NOTE: This is a nice chunky soup, but if you have any additional favorite vegetables, go ahead and add them, too.

BLACK BEAN SOUP

6 TO 8 SERVINGS

It's quick, easy, light, protein-rich. . . . Is there no end to the great things about this soup? Well, not till you reach the bottom of the bowl!

2 cans (10½ ounces each) condensed chicken broth	4 cans (15 ounces each) black beans, undrained
3 cups water	1 jar (16 ounces) salsa
1 medium-sized onion, chopped	½ teaspoon ground cumin

In a soup pot, combine the broth, water, and onion over medium heat. Cook for 5 minutes, or until the onions are tender, then reduce the heat to medium-low. In a blender, purée 2 cans of the black beans, with their liquid, until smooth. Add to the soup pot along with the remaining undrained beans. Stir in the salsa and cumin and simmer for 10 minutes, or until thoroughly heated, stirring occasionally.

NOTE: This is really nice topped with sour cream or shredded Monterey Jack cheese.

FIESTA SOUP

4 TO 6 SERVINGS

No need to plan a fiesta when you want to serve this soup, 'cause anytime you make it, it's fiesta time!

1 tablespoon butter
2 medium-sized green or red bell peppers (or 1 of each), diced
2 cans (10¾ ounces each) condensed cream of potato soup

1½ cups milk
½ cup picante sauce
½ teaspoon ground cumin
2 cups (8 ounces) shredded Mexican cheese blend

In a large saucepan, melt the butter over medium-high heat. Add the bell peppers and sauté for 5 to 6 minutes, or until tender. Reduce the heat to medium and add the remaining ingredients except the cheese. Cook for 3 to 5 minutes, or until heated through, stirring frequently; do not boil. Stir in the cheese until melted, then serve immediately.

NOTE: Garnish with some chopped fresh parsley or an additional spoonful of picante sauce in the center of each bowl.

ZINGY GAZPACHO

4 TO 6 SERVINGS

A cool classic that never goes out of style.

3 cups vegetable juice
1 jar (16 ounces) picante sauce
1 medium-sized tomato, diced
½ a medium-sized green bell
   pepper, diced

½ a medium-sized cucumber,
   diced
2 scallions, thinly sliced
1 cup sour cream (optional)

In a large bowl, combine all the ingredients except the sour cream; mix well. Cover and chill for at least 2 hours, or until ready to serve. Serve each bowl topped with a dollop of sour cream, if desired.

NOTE: If you want to give this some real zing, start off with a spicy-style vegetable juice. It's the perfect soup to make ahead and have on hand, since it'll last for a few days in the fridge.

MEXICAN CAESAR SALAD

6 TO 8 SERVINGS

Did you know that traditional Caesar salad has nothing to do with Julius Caesar? Nope. It actually originated in Mexico. And this version gives it more typically Mexican flavor.

1 large head romaine lettuce, cut into bite-sized pieces
1 cup coarsely crushed tortilla chips
¼ cup grated Parmesan cheese
⅓ cup mayonnaise

¼ cup milk
2 tablespoons lime juice
2 tablespoons dry taco seasoning mix
2 teaspoons Dijon-style mustard

In a large bowl, combine the lettuce, chips, and Parmesan cheese. In a small bowl, whisk together the remaining ingredients until well blended. Pour over the lettuce mixture and toss until well coated and combined. Serve immediately.

NOTE: For an authentic Mexican flavor, substitute grated Cotija cheese for the Parmesan cheese. Cotija can usually be found in specialty cheese departments.

SPICY SHRIMP SALAD

6 TO 8 SERVINGS

Dressing sure can make the salad—and with this recipe I've created a spicy dressing and salad combination that should be a nice all-in-one change of pace.

1 package (3 ounces) cream cheese, softened
⅔ cup mayonnaise
⅓ cup picante sauce
1 teaspoon prepared white horseradish

1 can (4 ounces) chopped green chilies, drained
1 can (6 ounces) shrimp, rinsed and drained
1 medium-sized head iceberg lettuce, shredded

In a medium-sized bowl, with an electric beater on medium speed, beat the cream cheese and mayonnaise until smooth. Add the picante sauce and horseradish and continue beating until well blended. With a spoon, stir in the chilies and shrimp, reserving a few shrimp for garnish; mix well. Cover and chill until ready to serve. To serve, place the shredded lettuce on a large platter or in individual serving bowls and top with the shrimp mixture. Garnish with the reserved shrimp and serve.

NOTE: Remember, the spiciness of this salad will depend upon the spiciness of the picante sauce you use.

TACO SALAD

8 TO 12 SERVINGS

Every time I serve this salad, everybody loves it so much they just can't seem to get enough! And not only does it taste great, it looks great, too.

1 pound ground beef
1 package (1¼ ounces) dry taco seasoning mix
1 medium-sized head iceberg lettuce, chopped
2 cups (8 ounces) shredded Cheddar cheese
1 can (15 ounces) kidney beans, rinsed and drained

2 large tomatoes, diced
1 can (4 ounces) sliced black olives, drained
1 bag (14½ ounces) ranch-flavored tortilla chips, crushed
1 bottle (16 ounces) sweet-and-spicy French salad dressing

In a medium-sized skillet, brown the ground beef and taco seasoning mix over medium-high heat, stirring to break up the meat; drain and cool. In an extra-large glass salad bowl, layer half of the lettuce, then half of the cheese, beans, ground beef mixture, tomatoes, and olives. Repeat the layers once more, then top with the crushed tortilla chips. Drizzle with dressing as desired, and serve.

NOTE: Serve this in Tortilla Bowls (page 88) for totally edible individual salads—bowls and all!

45

QUICK STEAK SALAD

6 TO 8 SERVINGS

In America, we traditionally eat our salad before our main course. And in Europe, salad is usually served *after* the main course. Well, with this dish, it doesn't matter where you're from, 'cause you get your salad and main course all in one.

1 tablespoon chili powder
½ teaspoon ground cumin
½ teaspoon salt
¼ teaspoon cayenne pepper
One 2-pound boneless beef
   sirloin steak, about 1½ inches
   thick, trimmed

1 medium-sized head iceberg
   lettuce, shredded
1 can (15 ounces) black beans,
   rinsed and drained
1 cup salsa

Preheat the broiler. In a small bowl, combine the chili powder, cumin, salt, and cayenne pepper. Rub over the entire surface of the steak; discard any leftover seasoning mixture. Place the meat on a broiler pan and broil for 18 to 20 minutes for medium-rare, or to desired doneness, turning halfway through the broiling. Remove from the broiler and let stand for 10 minutes. Place the shredded lettuce on a large serving platter or on individual serving plates. In a small bowl, combine the beans and salsa and spoon evenly over the lettuce. Slice the steak across the grain into thin slices and place evenly over the salad. Serve immediately.

PAELLA SALAD

4 TO 6 SERVINGS

A little Spanish, a little Mexican . . . and a lot of taste!

1 package (10 ounces) yellow rice
2 tablespoons red wine vinegar
⅓ cup vegetable oil
⅛ teaspoon dry mustard
1 large tomato, chopped
½ cup finely chopped onion

½ a medium-sized red bell pepper,
 chopped
1½ teaspoons salt
1 package (10 ounces) frozen
 cooked shrimp, thawed

Cook the rice according to the package directions; set aside to cool. In a large bowl, combine the remaining ingredients except the shrimp; mix well. Add the cooled rice and shrimp; toss to coat well. Cover and chill for at least 2 hours before serving.

NOTE: For additional color and flavor, add a thawed 10-ounce package of frozen peas to the salad when tossing.

RANCH POTATO SALAD

14 TO 16 SERVINGS

Down on the ranch or at a picnic in the park, everybody will appreciate this flavorful potato salad.

4 pounds red-skinned potatoes,
    washed
6 hard-boiled eggs, chopped
1 medium-sized red bell pepper,
    minced
4 celery stalks, diced

2 cups mayonnaise
1 can (4 ounces) chopped green
    chilies, drained
1½ teaspoons chili powder
1 teaspoon salt
½ teaspoon black pepper

Place the potatoes in a large pot, then add enough water to cover them completely. Bring to a boil over high heat and cook for 25 to 30 minutes, or until the potatoes are fork-tender. Drain and let cool slightly. Cut the potatoes into 1-inch chunks and place in a large bowl; add the remaining ingredients and mix gently until the potatoes are completely coated. Serve warm, or cover and chill until ready to serve.

NOTE: This recipe makes a really large batch, so, after your get-together, you can keep any leftovers in a covered container in the refrigerator. I could almost guarantee that before you know it, it'll all disappear (at least that's what happens when I leave it in *my* refrigerator).

MEXICAN JUMPING BEAN SALAD

8 TO 12 SERVINGS

Have you ever seen Mexican jumping beans? They're amazing! And so is this salad, so wait till you see it practically jump out of the bowl onto people's plates. I bet that'll have you jumping for joy!

3 cups cold cooked white rice
1 can (16 ounces) kidney beans, rinsed and drained
1 can (15 ounces) garbanzo beans (chick peas), rinsed and drained
2 cans (4 ounces each) chopped green chilies
1 package (10 ounces) frozen peas, thawed and drained

3 celery stalks, chopped
1 medium-sized red onion, chopped
¼ cup chopped fresh cilantro
⅔ cup Garlic-Garlic Dressing (see page 50) or bottled Italian dressing

In a large bowl, combine all the ingredients except the dressing. Add the dressing and toss gently to coat well. Cover and chill for at least 2 hours, or until ready to serve.

NOTE: I like to make this salad the night before I plan to serve it so that the dressing flavors can really permeate the rice and beans.

GARLIC-GARLIC DRESSING

ABOUT 1⅓ CUPS

Yup, the title is correct. There's a load of garlic in this dressing . . . so be sure to share it with the ones you love!

⅔ cup white vinegar
½ cup olive or vegetable oil
¼ cup water
4 garlic cloves, minced

1 teaspoon garlic powder
1½ teaspoons salt
1 teaspoon black pepper

In a medium-sized bowl, whisk together all the ingredients until well blended. Serve immediately, or place in an airtight container and chill until ready to use.

NOTE: The reason I use fresh garlic *and* garlic powder in here is that the garlic powder flavors the dressing throughout, while the fresh garlic adds great flavor *and* texture.

SNAPPY SOUTHWEST DRESSING

ABOUT 2 CUPS

It's so easy to make, you can practically whip up a batch before you can say "creamy, spicy dressing" three times. Go ahead, try it!

1 cup picante sauce
1 cup sour cream

¼ teaspoon chili powder
¼ teaspoon ground cumin

Place all the ingredients in a medium-sized bowl and mix until well combined. Serve immediately, or cover and chill until ready to use.

NOTE: This dressing is a perfect complement to any salad, and it can even be used as a substitute for salsa and sour cream in tacos or fajitas.

BRUNCH/
ALMUERZO

BANDITO BRUNCH

12 TO 15 SERVINGS

Wanna add some excitement to your next brunch? Then get ready to shake those maracas and click the castanets, 'cause before you know it, all the banditos will be lining up at your table.

1 pound bulk pork sausage
1 tablespoon chopped fresh
  jalapeño pepper
1 can (17.3 ounces) refrigerated
  buttermilk biscuits

1 can (10.8 ounces) refrigerated
  buttermilk biscuits
2 cups (8 ounces) shredded
  Mexican cheese blend

Preheat the oven to 375°F. In a medium-sized skillet, brown the sausage for 7 to 8 minutes over medium-high heat. Stir in the jalapeño and remove from the heat. Separate the biscuit dough into a total of 13 biscuits. Cut each biscuit into 6 pieces and place in a large bowl; add the sausage mixture and the cheese and toss until well blended. Spoon into a 9" × 13" baking dish that has been coated with nonstick vegetable spray and bake for 30 to 35 minutes, or until the biscuits are golden and cooked through.

NOTE: Make sure to buy bulk sausage, or remove the casing from your favorite type of link sausage. Even turkey sausage will work.

STUFFED CHILIES SOUFFLÉ

9 TO 12 SERVINGS

Chiles rellenos, which means "stuffed chilies," is a popular dish in Mexico. The traditional dish is really tasty, so, with our busy schedules these days, I decided to keep the taste but make it into a quick soufflé instead of time-consuming individual servings.

4 cans (4 ounces each) whole green chilies, drained, patted dry, and cut lengthwise in half
4 cups (16 ounces) shredded Monterey Jack cheese
1 small onion, diced
4 eggs
1 can (5 ounces) evaporated milk

Preheat the oven to 350°F. Spread half of the chilies over the bottom of a 9" × 13" baking dish that has been coated with nonstick vegetable spray. Top with the cheese, then with the onion. Cover with the remaining chilies. In a medium-sized bowl, whisk together the eggs and evaporated milk; pour over the chilies. Cover tightly with aluminum foil and bake for 40 minutes. Remove the aluminum foil and bake for 18 to 20 more minutes, or until golden and set. Cool for 3 to 4 minutes before cutting and serving.

NOTE: If you'd rather, shredded Cheddar cheese or even a blend of cheeses can be substituted for the Monterey Jack cheese.

BREAKFAST BURRITOS

10 BURRITOS

Eggs, meat, vegetables, and bread all rolled into one. Now that's *my* idea of a breakfast on the go!

Ten 8-inch flour tortillas
2 tablespoons butter
1 medium-sized onion, chopped
2 medium-sized green or red bell peppers (or 1 of each), chopped
1 package (8 ounces) precooked sausage links, cut into ¼-inch slices

10 eggs
½ cup milk
½ teaspoon salt
½ teaspoon black pepper
1½ cups (6 ounces) shredded Mexican cheese blend

Preheat the oven to 200°F. Tightly wrap the tortillas in foil and place in the oven for about 15 minutes to warm. Meanwhile, in a large skillet, melt the butter over medium-high heat. Sauté the onion and bell peppers for 6 to 8 minutes, or until tender. Stir in the sausage and sauté for 4 minutes. In a large bowl, combine the eggs, milk, salt, and black pepper; whisk until thoroughly combined. Pour into the skillet over the sausage and vegetables and cook for 4 to 5 minutes, until the eggs are scrambled and just set. Add the cheese and stir to blend thoroughly. Remove the tortillas from the oven. Place ½ cup of the egg mixture down the center of each tortilla, roll up, and place seam side down on a serving platter. Serve immediately.

NOTE: You can prepare these ahead of time, place the finished burritos in a baking dish, cover with aluminum foil, and keep in a warm oven until ready to serve.

HUEVOS RANCHEROS

6 SERVINGS

You've seen this listed on brunch menus in lots of restaurants around the country. Now, don't let the name scare you. It's really just eggs, cheese, and salsa served in a tortilla.

2 tablespoons vegetable oil
Six 6-inch corn tortillas
1½ cups salsa
1 tablespoon butter

6 eggs
¾ cup (3 ounces) shredded
    Monterey Jack cheese

In a large skillet, heat the oil over medium heat. Heat the tortillas in the skillet, one at a time, for 8 to 10 seconds, or until soft. Drain on paper towels. Place on individual serving plates and spoon ¼ cup of the salsa into the center of each tortilla; set aside. Drain the oil from the skillet, then melt the butter over medium heat. Crack the eggs into the skillet, without breaking the yolks, and fry for 4 to 5 minutes, or to desired doneness. (Depending on the size of your eggs and your skillet, you may need to cook this in batches.) Place one egg on top of each tortilla and sprinkle the eggs evenly with the cheese. (The heat of the eggs will melt the cheese.) Serve immediately.

NOTE: Although it's not the traditional way to serve these, if you prefer, you can scramble your eggs instead of frying them whole and even mix the cheese in with the scrambled eggs instead of sprinkling it on top.

TORTILLA BLINTZES

12 BLINTZES

Tortilla *blintzes*?! Am I kidding? Nope! I love to mix and match the foods of different cultures, so why not make cheese-stuffed tortillas that can be the perfect addition to any brunch buffet?

1 container (16 ounces) small-curd cottage cheese	⅓ cup sugar
1 package (3 ounces) cream cheese, softened	1 egg
	Twelve 6-inch flour tortillas

Preheat the oven to 400°F. In a large bowl, combine all the ingredients except the tortillas; mix well. Place ¼ cup of the mixture in the center of each tortilla. Fold the bottom of each tortilla up over the cheese mixture, then fold both sides over, envelope fashion. Fold the top of each tortilla closed and place seam side down in a 9" × 13" baking dish that has been coated with nonstick vegetable spray. Bake for 12 to 15 minutes, or until slightly golden. Serve immediately.

NOTE: Top with sour cream or your favorite fruit preserves.

BORDER BISCUIT BAKE

12 TO 15 SERVINGS

Keep this recipe handy for those weekends when a special brunch is planned, especially when company is expected!

1 can (17.3 ounces) refrigerated buttermilk biscuits
1 can (10.8 ounces) refrigerated buttermilk biscuits
1 jar (16 ounces) salsa
3 cups (12 ounces) shredded Monterey Jack cheese
1 medium-sized green bell pepper, chopped
3 scallions, sliced
1 can (2¼ ounces) sliced black olives, drained

Preheat the oven to 375°F. Separate the biscuit dough into a total of 13 biscuits. Cut each biscuit into 6 pieces. Place in a large bowl and add the salsa; toss to coat well. Spoon the mixture into a 9" × 13" baking dish that has been coated with nonstick vegetable spray. Sprinkle with the cheese, bell pepper, scallions, and olives. Bake for 35 to 45 minutes, or until the edges are golden brown and the center is set. Remove from the oven and let stand for 15 minutes before cutting into squares.

NOTE: This "bake" is a perfect replacement for rolls, or simply for a bread and vegetable side dish in one. Serve it with additional salsa, if desired.

GREEN CHILI PIE

6 TO 8 SERVINGS

Simply combine, blend, pour, and bake. Yup, this is probably the most unusual pie you've ever served . . . and your family will love you for it!

1 cup heavy cream

3 eggs

2 cups (8 ounces) shredded
   Cheddar cheese

1 can (4 ounces) chopped green
   chilies, drained

½ cup chopped red onion

½ cup biscuit baking mix

¼ teaspoon salt

Preheat the oven to 350°F. Combine all the ingredients in a blender and blend for 20 to 30 seconds, until well blended. Pour into a 9-inch pie plate that has been coated with nonstick vegetable spray. Bake on the middle oven rack for 40 to 45 minutes, or until the top is golden and the center is set.

NOTE: If you make this ahead of time and freeze it, you can just thaw and reheat it when guests are expected.

SMOKED SALMON ROLL-UPS

ABOUT 4 DOZEN

With this recipe, we tell the bagel to move over and let the tortilla take center stage. And these are really as much fun to make as they are to eat.

1 container (8 ounces) whipped cream cheese
¼ cup sour cream
1 teaspoon dried dillweed
1 teaspoon lemon juice

3 ounces smoked salmon, finely diced
Eight 6-inch flour tortillas
8 scallions, trimmed to 6-inch lengths

In a medium-sized bowl, combine the cream cheese, sour cream, dillweed, lemon juice, and salmon; mix well. Spread evenly over the tortillas. Place a scallion across the bottom edge of each tortilla and roll up tightly; place seam side down on a serving plate. Cover and chill for at least 2 hours, or until ready to serve. Cut into 1-inch slices and serve.

NOTE: To get more of the smoked salmon flavor, instead of dicing the salmon, prepare the cream cheese mixture without the salmon and spread it on the tortillas. Top each tortilla with thin slices of salmon, then a scallion, and roll as directed.

MEXICAN TOAST

4 SERVINGS

Here's the long-lost cousin of French toast. I especially like it 'cause you can pick it up and eat it with your fingers . . . without feeling guilty!

2 eggs
⅓ cup milk
2 tablespoons sugar
¼ teaspoon ground cinnamon
¼ teaspoon vanilla extract

Four 10-inch flour tortillas
¼ cup (½ stick) butter, divided
3 tablespoons confectioners' sugar

In a medium-sized bowl, whisk the eggs, milk, sugar, cinnamon, and vanilla until well blended. Cut each tortilla into quarters, then place in the egg mixture. Gently stir to completely coat the tortillas. Allow to soak for 10 minutes, or until softened. In a large skillet, melt 1 tablespoon butter over medium-high heat. Add 4 tortilla quarters and cook for 4 to 5 minutes, or until golden, turning halfway through the cooking. Drain on paper towels. Repeat with the remaining butter and tortillas. Sprinkle with the confectioners' sugar and serve immediately.

NOTE: Sure, you can top these with maple syrup, or even fresh or thawed frozen strawberries.

EASY CORN FRITTERS

ABOUT 2 DOZEN

This recipe is a take-off on a traditional American classic. I've made it as easy as possible 'cause, after all, isn't that what today's cooking is all about?

1¾ cups all-purpose flour
2 teaspoons baking powder
2 teaspoons salt
½ teaspoon black pepper
2 eggs, beaten
¼ cup salsa

1 can (14¾ ounces) cream-style corn
1 can (14½ ounces) whole kernel corn, drained
¼ cup vegetable oil, or more as needed

In a large bowl, combine the flour, baking powder, salt, and pepper. Add the eggs and salsa; mix well. Stir in the cream-style and whole kernel corn. Heat 1 tablespoon oil in a large skillet over medium heat. Drop the batter into the hot skillet 1 tablespoonful at a time and cook for 4 to 5 minutes, until the fritters are golden, turning halfway through the cooking. Remove to a covered platter. Add 1 tablespoon oil to the skillet. When hot, repeat with the remaining batter, adding more oil as needed.

NOTE: These can be served with an omelet, instead of home fries, or as an appetizer by themselves or with warm salsa for dipping.

SOUTH-OF-THE-BORDER CHEESE PIE

8 TO 12 SERVINGS

When you can make this combination of great tastes right at home, there's no need to head south of the border!

4 eggs, beaten
1 cup (½ pint) heavy cream
2 cups (8 ounces) shredded
   Mexican cheese blend
1 can (11 ounces) Mexican-style
   corn, drained

¼ cup real bacon bits
2 teaspoons chili powder
Two 9-inch frozen pie shells,
   thawed

Preheat the oven to 375°F. In a medium-sized bowl, combine all the ingredients except the pie shells. Pour the mixture into the 2 pie shells, distributing it evenly. Bake for 35 to 40 minutes, or until a knife inserted in the middle of the pie comes out clean and the top is golden brown. Allow to stand for 5 minutes before cutting and serving.

NOTE: If you have leftover cooked bacon, just crumble 4 or 5 strips and use it in place of the bacon bits.

CHEESY SPOON BREAD

4 TO 6 SERVINGS

Put away your bread knife—there's no slicing this bread. Just spoon it out. And since the butter is baked in, you won't need a butter knife, either!

½ cup fine white cornmeal
  (see Note)
1 cup boiling water
2 tablespoons butter
1½ teaspoons baking powder
½ teaspoon salt
¼ teaspoon black pepper

3 eggs
½ cup milk
1 can (4 ounces) chopped green
  chilies, drained
1 cup (4 ounces) shredded
  Mexican cheese blend

Preheat the oven to 400°F. In a medium-sized bowl, with an electric beater on medium speed, beat the cornmeal, water, butter, baking powder, salt, and pepper for 30 seconds. Add the eggs and milk and beat for 1 to 2 minutes, or until thoroughly mixed. Pour half of the batter into a 9" × 5" loaf pan that has been coated with nonstick vegetable spray. Spoon the chilies and ⅔ cup cheese evenly over the batter. Pour the remaining batter over the cheese and top with the remaining ⅓ cup cheese. Bake for 20 to 25 minutes, or until golden. Serve warm.

NOTE: Fine white cornmeal is available in the supermarket baking aisle or alongside the hot cereals.

MEXICANA BAGELS

12 SERVINGS

In my other books, I've topped bagels with everything from vegetable cream cheese to happy faces. Now it's time to give them a bit of Mexican flair.

6 bagels, split
1 package (8 ounces) cream
  cheese, softened

¼ cup salsa
1 package (3 ounces) cooked
  chorizo sausage, chopped

Preheat the broiler. Place the bagel halves on a large rimmed baking sheet. In a medium-sized bowl, combine the cream cheese and salsa until well blended. Top the bagel halves evenly with the cream cheese mixture. Sprinkle with the sausage and broil for 3 to 4 minutes, or until thoroughly heated.

NOTE: For appetizer-sized treats, substitute a 9-ounce package of frozen mini-bagels, thawed and split, for the full-sized bagels.

JALAPEÑO JELLY

6 CUPS

Homemade jelly can be so easy! And this one's both sweet and spicy for a nice change of pace.

2 medium-sized green bell peppers, chopped
14 fresh jalapeño peppers (about ½ pound), stems and seeds removed, chopped
7 cups sugar

1¼ cups apple cider vinegar
⅓ cup apple juice
1 package (6 ounces) liquid pectin
¼ teaspoon green food color (optional)

In a soup pot, combine all the ingredients except the pectin and food color. Bring to a rolling boil over medium heat and boil for 2 to 3 minutes. Add the pectin, return the mixture to a boil, and boil for 2 to 3 more minutes, stirring constantly. Remove from the heat and strain, discarding the pepper pieces. Place in a large bowl and add the food color, if desired; mix until well blended. Pour into clean airtight glass or plastic containers and allow to jell at room temperature. Store in the refrigerator. (It should last for months this way.)

NOTE: My favorite way to eat this jelly is on a cracker with cream cheese. Oh—liquid pectin can be found in the supermarket produce section or near the jellies and jams or the baking ingredients.

TORTILLAS/
TORTILLAS

the **T**ortilla **W**orkout

taco
sit-up

quesadilla
stretch

enchilada
curl

TORTILLAS

Wow! A whole chapter built around tortillas! Well, of course—tortillas are a building block for so many Mexican foods. In southern Mexico, corn tortillas are the most prevalent, and in northern Mexico, flour tortillas are popular, due to the abundance of wheat. With the burst of Tex-Mex cooking in the United States in recent years, corn and flour tortillas can be found in supermarkets across the country—in many forms, from fresh and canned ones to refrigerated and frozen ones. And, sure, you can even make your own. See my easy recipes on pages 89 and 90.

Boy, are tortillas versatile! They're simply thin dough rounds that are quick-cooked on an ungreased hot surface. And you can roll, fill, fold, bake, warm . . . do almost anything with them! That's why I've included this list of common foods that are all based on tortillas. It should help clear up any confusion you may have about the differences among these items.

Burrito—a tortilla wrapped around a filling and baked until warmed through.

Chimichanga—a tortilla filled and folded envelope-style, then fried or baked.

Enchilada—a tortilla rolled around a filling, then baked in a sauce and/or served with a red chili sauce.

Quesadilla—two tortillas layered with cheese and grilled or fried.

Taco—a tortilla wrapped around a cooked meat, chicken, or other type of filling. Corn tortillas are often fried in a U-shape for ease in filling and making crispy tacos. Flour tortillas are usually simply warmed before filling, resulting in soft tacos.

Tostada—a tortilla warmed or toasted and piled with a selection of toppings, including cheese, cooked meat, veggies, or beans. Similar to a small pizza.

Tostadita—a tortilla cut into triangles and fried until crisp. (Tortilla Crisps, page 87, are really baked tostaditas.)

  71

CANTINA BURRITOS

4 BURRITOS

Not all burritos are filled with a mixture containing either meat or chicken. Take this one, for instance. It's brimming with rice, beans, and a whole lot of flavor.

1½ cups cooked white rice
1 can (16 ounces) pinto beans,
    rinsed and drained (see Note)
1 medium-sized ripe tomato,
    chopped
⅓ cup salsa

½ teaspoon onion powder
1 cup (4 ounces) shredded
    Mexican cheese blend
Four 10-inch flour tortillas
1 cup shredded iceberg lettuce

In a medium-sized saucepan, combine the rice, beans, tomato, salsa, and onion powder over medium heat. Cook for 4 to 5 minutes, or until heated through. Remove from the heat and add the cheese; mix well. Spoon the bean mixture evenly onto the centers of the tortillas and top each with ¼ cup lettuce. Fold the bottom of each tortilla up over the bean mixture, then fold both sides over, envelope fashion. Fold the top of each tortilla closed and turn seam side down. Serve immediately.

NOTE: Red beans, black beans, pinto beans—whichever are your favorites are the ones to use.

BLT BURRITOS

4 BURRITOS

Bacon, lettuce, and tomato—one of the all-time favorite lunch combos. Now you can mix it up, roll it up, and enjoy it in one easy-to-eat package.

4 cups shredded iceberg lettuce	⅔ cup real bacon bits
1 medium-sized ripe tomato, chopped	¼ teaspoon salt
	⅛ teaspoon black pepper
1 cup mayonnaise	Four 10-inch flour tortillas

In a large bowl, combine the lettuce, tomato, mayonnaise, bacon bits, salt, and pepper; mix well. Spoon the mixture evenly onto the centers of the tortillas. Fold the bottom of each tortilla up over the vegetable mixture, then fold both sides over, envelope fashion. Fold the top of each tortilla closed and turn seam side down. Serve immediately.

NOTE: If I don't have bacon bits on hand, I chop a quarter pound of deli turkey and mix it in to create a "TLT" burrito.

BEEFY BURRITOS

4 BURRITOS

Don't think of this one as lightweight . . . uh-uh! Sure, it could be a snack or lunch, but you could say I "beefed" it up to make it work as a hearty dinner, too.

1 pound ground beef
1 small onion, chopped
1 garlic clove, minced
½ teaspoon chili powder
¼ teaspoon ground cumin
½ teaspoon salt
1 package (10 ounces) frozen
    chopped spinach, thawed and
    squeezed dry

1½ cups (6 ounces) shredded
    Monterey Jack cheese
Four 10-inch flour tortillas,
    warmed

In a large nonstick skillet, brown the ground beef, onion, and garlic over medium heat for 7 to 10 minutes, or until the beef is no longer pink, stirring occasionally. Drain off the excess liquid and stir in the chili powder, cumin, and salt. Stir in the spinach and heat through. Remove from the heat and stir in the cheese. Spoon the mixture evenly onto the centers of the warmed tortillas. Fold the bottom of each tortilla up over the beef mixture, then fold both sides over, envelope fashion. Fold the top of each tortilla closed and turn seam side down. Serve immediately.

NOTE: Serve topped with warmed salsa or any of your favorite toppings. Check out all of the possibilities on pages xv to xvii.

GARDEN BURRITOS

8 BURRITOS

Fresh-from-the garden flavor, with fresh-from-the garden ingredients, makes for an easy way to get your family to eat their vegetables.

1 package (6 ounces) alfalfa
  sprouts
2 large ripe tomatoes, chopped
1 large cucumber, peeled and
  chopped

Eight 10-inch flour tortillas
½ cup sour cream
½ cup salsa

Lay the tortillas on a work surface. Divide the alfalfa sprouts, tomatoes, and cucumbers evenly among the centers of the tortillas. In a small bowl, combine the sour cream and salsa; mix well. Dollop the mixture evenly over the vegetables. Fold the bottom of each tortilla up over the vegetable mixture, then fold both sides over, envelope fashion. Fold the top of each tortilla closed and turn seam side down. Serve immediately, or cover and chill until ready to serve.

NOTE: Sometimes I add roasted peppers or slices of jalapeño peppers for a little variety.

MUY BUENO TACOS

12 TACOS

When you think of Mexican food, you probably think of tacos that are crispy on the outside and flavorful on the inside. Here you go. . . . Sometimes the simplest things are the best!

1 to 1½ pounds ground beef
1 large onion, chopped, divided
½ a medium-sized green bell
   pepper, chopped
2 tablespoons Taco Seasoning
   (page 14)
½ cup picante sauce

12 taco shells
1 to 2 cups shredded iceberg
   lettuce
1 cup (4 ounces) shredded
   Cheddar cheese
1 cup chopped ripe tomatoes

Preheat the oven to 350°F. In a large skillet, brown the ground beef, ½ cup onions, and the bell pepper over medium heat for 8 to 10 minutes, or until no pink remains in the beef. Drain off the excess liquid and stir in the Taco Seasoning and picante sauce; mix well. Reduce the heat to low and simmer for 3 to 4 minutes; remove from the heat. Meanwhile, place the taco shells on a cookie sheet and bake for 5 to 7 minutes, or until crisp. Remove from the oven and fill each shell one-third full with the meat mixture, then top with the remaining onion, the lettuce, cheese, and tomatoes.

NOTE: You can also top each of these with a dollop of sour cream or guacamole, if you'd like.

CHICKEN SALAD TACOS

8 TACOS

It seems as if most restaurants and delis serve chicken salad these days. So we can find it on almost everything from hero or submarine rolls to bagels and even focaccia. But I haven't found one yet that serves it like this . . . taco style. Who knows? It might be the next food fad!

1 can (10 ounces) chunk white
    chicken, drained and flaked
1 celery stalk, chopped
⅓ cup salsa
¼ cup sour cream
1 teaspoon ground cumin

8 taco shells
1 cup shredded iceberg lettuce
1 small ripe tomato, chopped
½ cup (2 ounces) shredded
    Cheddar cheese

In a medium-sized bowl, combine the chicken, celery, salsa, sour cream, and cumin; mix well. Spoon evenly into the taco shells. Top with the lettuce, tomato, and cheese; serve immediately.

NOTE: You can prepare the chicken salad and chop the vegetables ahead of time, then keep them chilled. That way, you're all ready for a quick and easy meal!

TORTILLA DOGS

8 TORTILLA DOGS

When the heat of the summer gives us lazy, "dog day" afternoons, here's the answer to creating a quick meal that's doggone tasty!

1½ pounds ground beef
1 package (1¼ ounces) dry taco
    seasoning mix
¾ cup water

8 hot dogs (about 1 pound)
Eight 6- or 8-inch flour tortillas
1 cup (4 ounces) shredded
    Mexican cheese blend

In a large skillet, brown the ground beef for 4 to 5 minutes over medium-high heat. Add the taco seasoning and water and bring to a boil. Reduce the heat to medium and cook for 12 to 15 minutes, or until the liquid evaporates, stirring occasionally. Meanwhile, in another skillet, brown the hot dogs over medium heat, turning frequently. Divide the mixture evenly among the centers of the tortillas and sprinkle with the cheese; top each with a hot dog. Roll the tortillas around the hot dogs and place seam side down on a serving plate. Serve immediately.

NOTE: If you want, you can make these in advance, place them in a baking dish, cover with aluminum foil, and set in a 200°F. oven for 1 to 2 hours before serving.

CHICKEN TORTILLA CAKE

4 TO 6 SERVINGS

Want to get the family to the dinner table in a hurry? Just tell them they're having cake for dinner. Hey, it looks like a cake, and it'll be just as popular!

½ cup vegetable oil
Six 8-inch flour tortillas
1 cup sour cream
¾ teaspoon hot pepper sauce
½ teaspoon dry fajita seasoning mix

2½ cups shredded cooked chicken
4 cups (16 ounces) shredded
    Colby-Jack cheese blend
6 scallions, chopped
1½ tablespoons butter, melted

Preheat the oven to 400°F. In a large skillet, heat the oil over medium-high heat (or heat to 375°F. in an electric skillet). Fry the tortillas, one at a time, for 10 to 15 seconds, or until golden brown. Drain well on paper towels. In a medium-sized bowl, combine the sour cream, hot sauce, and fajita seasoning; mix well. Place 1 tortilla on a large rimmed baking sheet that has been coated with nonstick vegetable spray, then spread 1 tablespoon of the sour cream mixture over the top. Sprinkle with ½ cup shredded chicken, ¾ cup cheese, and one sixth of the scallions. Place a tortilla on top and repeat the layers 4 more times, ending with a plain tortilla on top. Cover and refrigerate the remaining sour cream mixture. Brush the tops and sides of the tortilla cake with the melted butter, then cover tightly with aluminum foil and bake for 25 minutes. Remove the foil and place on a serving plate. Spread the top tortilla with the remaining sour cream mixture and top with the remaining cheese and chopped scallion. Cut into wedges and serve immediately.

NOTE: Two 10-ounce cans of chunk white chicken, drained and flaked, can be substituted for the shredded cooked chicken.

 79

FLAUTAS

8 FLAUTAS

In Spanish, *flauta* means flute or flute-shaped. In this book, it refers to a Mexican roll-up worthy of a grand "*Olé!*"

1 can (16 ounces) refried beans
1 can (4 ounces) chopped green chilies, drained
½ a small onion, chopped
1 cup (4 ounces) shredded Cheddar cheese

¼ cup chopped toasted almonds
1 tablespoon dried cilantro
Eight 6- or 8-inch flour tortillas
2 tablespoons vegetable oil, divided

Preheat the oven to 425°F. In a large skillet, combine the beans, chilies, onion, cheese, almonds, and cilantro over medium heat. Cook for 3 to 5 minutes, or until the mixture is hot and the cheese is melted. Spoon the bean mixture horizontally across the bottom edge of each tortilla, distributing evenly, and roll up tightly to close, forming a flute shape. Place seam side down on a large rimmed baking sheet. Use 1 tablespoon of the oil to brush the tops of the tortillas; bake for 16 to 18 minutes, or until golden, brushing with the remaining 1 tablespoon oil halfway through the baking. Serve immediately.

NOTE: Serve topped with picante sauce, if desired.

SANTA FE CHICKEN TOSTADAS

6 TOSTADAS

Some folks say that tostadas are like open-faced tacos. Others say they're individual Mexican pizzas. I think they're all right. What about you?

2 teaspoons vegetable oil
4 boneless, skinless chicken
  breast halves (about 1 pound
  total), cut into 1-inch cubes
½ cup water
1 package (1¼ ounces) dry taco
  seasoning mix

1 can (15 ounces) black beans,
  rinsed and drained
¾ cup (3 ounces) shredded
  Mexican cheese blend, divided
Six 6-inch tostadas (see Note)
2 scallions, sliced

In a large nonstick skillet, heat the oil over medium heat. Add the chicken and sauté for 2 minutes, until browned. Add the water and taco seasoning; reduce the heat to low and simmer for 5 minutes. Add the black beans and simmer for 2 more minutes. Remove from the heat. Sprinkle the cheese evenly over the tostadas, top with the chicken mixture, and sprinkle with the scallions. Serve immediately.

NOTE: If ready-made tostadas aren't available, place six 6-inch corn tortillas on a baking sheet and bake in a 375°F. oven for 5 to 7 minutes, or until crisp.

PEPPER JACK QUESADILLAS

5 QUESADILLAS

If it's got cheese in it, you know I love it! And what could be cheesier than a quesadilla? Mmm!

2½ cups (10 ounces) shredded Monterey Jack–pepper cheese	Ten 10-inch flour tortillas 2½ teaspoons vegetable oil

Sprinkle ½ cup of the cheese over each of 5 tortillas and top with the remaining tortillas, making sandwiches. In a large skillet, heat ½ teaspoon oil over medium heat. Place 1 "tortilla sandwich" in the skillet and cook for 3 to 4 minutes, or until the cheese is melted, turning halfway through the cooking. Remove to a covered platter and continue with the remaining tortilla sandwiches until all are cooked. Cut each finished quesadilla into 4 wedges and serve.

NOTE: I like to serve these with sour cream, salsa, and sliced scallions. And for added cheese flavor, after the quesadilla has been turned over, I brush the top with an additional ½ teaspoon vegetable oil and sprinkle with a teaspoon of grated Parmesan cheese.

STEAK FAJITAS

6 FAJITAS

Now we're talking! This is one of my favorite ways to eat tortillas. Fajitas are great because you get to put exactly what you want in them. And steak fajitas are super because . . . well, because I love tender, marinated steak!

¼ cup vegetable oil, divided
Juice of 3 limes
1 teaspoon garlic powder
½ teaspoon salt
¼ teaspoon black pepper
One 1-pound beef skirt steak

3 medium-sized red, green, or yellow bell peppers (or 1 of each), cut into strips
3 medium-sized onions, cut into wedges
Six 8- or 10-inch flour tortillas, warmed

In a large shallow dish, combine 3 tablespoons of the oil, the lime juice, garlic powder, salt, and pepper. Add the steak and turn to coat with the marinade. Cover and marinate in the refrigerator for 1 hour. In a large skillet, heat the remaining 1 tablespoon oil over medium heat and sauté the peppers and onions for 12 to 14 minutes, or until tender and slightly browned. Meanwhile, place another skillet over medium heat; remove the steak from the marinade, discarding any excess marinade, and cook the steak for 10 to 12 minutes for medium, or to desired doneness, turning halfway through the cooking. Remove from the skillet and slice across the grain into thin strips. Divide the steak, peppers, and onions evenly among the tortillas and roll up, or prepare separate serving plates of each item and allow everyone to stuff and roll his or her own fajita.

continued

NOTE: Add some guacamole, sour cream, salsa, or any of your other favorite toppings to your "fajita bar." And don't forget to check out all the possible toppings on pages xv to xvii. Fajitas are even better when they're made with grilled meat, so instead of cooking the steak in a skillet, you can grill it to desired doneness.

EL PASO ENCHILADAS

12 ENCHILADAS

Chicken enchiladas are really popular in El Paso, and many of the local cooks have their own version. They're actually very easy to make, 'cause you can use leftover chicken and bottled enchilada sauce. So why not give this Texas favorite a try?

Twelve 8- to 10-inch
   corn tortillas
4 cups diced cooked chicken
2 cups (8 ounces) shredded

Mexican cheese blend, divided
1 small red onion, chopped
1 can (15 ounces) enchilada
   sauce, divided

Preheat the oven to 200°F. Tightly wrap the tortillas in aluminum foil and place in the oven to warm for 10 minutes. Remove from the oven and increase the temperature to 400°F. In a medium-sized bowl, combine the chicken, 1 cup cheese, the onion, and ¾ cup enchilada sauce; mix well. Divide the mixture evenly among the centers of the tortillas. Tightly roll up the tortillas and place seam side down in a 9" × 13" baking dish that has been coated with non-stick vegetable spray. Top with the remaining enchilada sauce and sprinkle with the remaining 1 cup cheese. Bake for 15 to 18 minutes, or until the cheese is melted and the enchiladas are heated through.

NOTE: When I'm looking for a change, I use my own Red Chili Sauce (page 7) in place of the enchilada sauce.

TURKEY CHIMICHANGAS

8 CHIMICHANGAS

I just love that name! Now, these may not sound easy, but they are . . . especially when you bake them instead of deep-frying them.

½ cup vegetable oil, divided
1 medium-sized onion, chopped
1 can (4 ounces) chopped green
    chilies, drained
¼ teaspoon minced garlic
½ teaspoon ground cumin

2½ cups shredded cooked turkey
Eight 10-inch flour tortillas
1 medium-sized ripe tomato,
    chopped
1 cup (4 ounces) shredded
    Mexican cheese blend

Preheat the oven to 425°F. In a medium-sized skillet, combine 2 tablespoons oil, the onion, chilies, garlic, and cumin over high heat. Cook for 3 to 4 minutes, or until the onions are tender. Add the turkey and cook for 2 to 3 minutes, or until thoroughly heated. Spoon the mixture evenly onto the centers of the tortillas, then top with the tomato and cheese. Fold the bottom of each tortilla up over the cheese, then fold both sides over, envelope fashion. Fold the top of each tortilla closed. Pour the remaining oil onto a large rimmed baking sheet and place the chimichangas seam side down on the baking sheet; using a pastry brush, thoroughly coat each with oil. Bake for 18 to 20 minutes, turning halfway through the baking. Serve immediately.

NOTE: You can use two 10-ounce cans of chunk white turkey, drained and flaked, in place of the shredded cooked turkey.

TORTILLA CRISPS

80 CRISPS

If you want some low-fat crunchy goodness that can be ready in a flash, here's how to do it. They're perfect for dipping, topping, or just plain eating.

Eight 10-inch flour tortillas   Nonstick vegetable spray

Preheat the oven to 425°F. Coat 2 large rimmed baking sheets with nonstick vegetable spray. Coat both sides of each tortilla with the spray. Cut each tortilla into 8 wedges. Place half the wedges on the baking sheets and bake for 6 to 8 minutes, or until golden. Transfer to a large platter and spread out to cool. Repeat with the remaining wedges. Serve immediately, or cool completely and store in an airtight container until ready to use.

NOTE: These days, nonstick vegetable sprays come in many different flavors, so each time you make these, you can accent them with a new flavor.

TORTILLA BOWLS

4 TORTILLA BOWLS

It's a completely edible bowl! Now that's what I call a revolution in dinnerware.

Four 10-inch flour tortillas, at   Nonstick vegetable spray
   room temperature

Preheat the oven to 425°F. Place 4 oven-proof soup bowls on a rimmed baking sheet. Coat both sides of each tortilla with nonstick vegetable spray. Carefully mold the tortillas into the bowls. Place another oven-proof bowl on top of each tortilla. (If you don't have 8 oven-proof bowls, bake these one or two at a time.) Bake for 7 to 9 minutes, or until the tortillas hold their shape. Carefully remove the top bowls and bake the tortillas (still in the bottom bowls) for 3 to 4 more minutes, or until the tortillas are golden and crisp. Remove the tortillas from the bowls and allow to cool on a wire rack. Fill with your favorite salad and serve immediately.

NOTE: You can stack the Taco Salad on page 45 in these edible bowls, or you can toss the salad first, then serve it in these.

FLOUR TORTILLAS

8 TORTILLAS

No ready-made tortillas on hand? No problem! Yeah, these are a little more work than store-bought, but they're worth it, 'cause with a few off-the-shelf ingredients, you can have fresh, warm, homemade tortillas in minutes.

2 cups all-purpose flour
¾ teaspoon salt

¼ cup vegetable shortening
½ cup warm water

In a medium-sized bowl, combine the flour and salt. With your fingertips, mix in the shortening. Add the water and mix until a dough forms. Knead the dough on a floured surface for about 3 minutes, or until smooth and elastic. Divide into 8 equal pieces and shape into balls. Place each ball between 2 sheets of waxed paper, and, using a rolling pin, roll each into an 8- to 10-inch circle. Heat a large skillet over medium-high heat. Place a tortilla in the skillet and cook for 30 to 40 seconds, until the top is bubbly and the bottom is flecked with brown spots. Flip the tortilla over and cook for 20 more seconds, or until the second side is flecked with brown spots. Remove to a covered plate and repeat with the remaining tortillas. Serve warm.

NOTE: After rolling out the dough, keep the uncooked tortillas between sheets of waxed paper until you're ready to cook them. That way, they won't stick together.

CORN TORTILLAS

1 DOZEN TORTILLAS

You haven't had corn tortillas like these unless you've been lucky enough to have them homemade. Wow! When you have the time, make them yourself. You'll notice the difference!

2 cups instant corn masa mix
(see Note)
1 cup plus 2 tablespoons warm
water

1 teaspoon salt

In a medium-sized bowl, combine all the ingredients; mix well with a spoon until the dough forms a ball. Add 1 tablespoon more water if the mixture is too dry. Divide into 12 equal pieces and shape into balls. Cut open the 3 sealed sides of a large resealable plastic storage bag, leaving the zippered side intact and closed. Place a ball of dough between the two pieces of plastic. Using a rolling pin, roll each ball into a 6-inch circle. Heat a medium-sized nonstick skillet over medium heat. Place a tortilla in the skillet and cook for 30 seconds, then turn the tortilla and cook for 1 more minute. Turn the tortilla again and cook for 30 more seconds, or until golden. Remove to a covered plate and repeat with the remaining tortillas. Serve warm.

NOTE: Corn masa mix is available in the ethnic foods section of the supermarket.

Keep the balls of dough covered until you're ready to roll them so they won't dry out.

HOMEMADE EMPANADA DOUGH

DOUGH FOR 16 EMPANADAS

If you stay away from making your own dough 'cause you think it's too difficult, here's a recipe that'll make you think again.

2½ cups all-purpose flour	½ cup milk
1 teaspoon sugar	½ cup (1 stick) butter, softened
1 teaspoon salt	1 egg

In a medium-sized bowl, combine the flour, the sugar, and salt; mix well. Add the milk, butter, and egg; mix well. Divide the dough into 16 pieces and roll into balls. On a lightly floured surface, use the palm of your hand to flatten each ball into a 4-inch circle. Fill with the desired filling and bake according to the filling directions.

NOTE: You can use this in place of the refrigerated pie crust in the Spicy Beef Empanadas on page 27. For a quick chicken filling, drain and flake two 10-ounce cans of chunk white chicken. Mix it with 1 cup of salsa and spoon the mixture evenly into the centers of the pieces of dough. Fold each in half, seal the edges firmly, and crimp the edges with the tines of a fork. Bake in a 375°F. oven for 25 to 30 minutes, or until golden.

MEATS/
CARNES

MEXICAN POT ROAST

4 TO 6 SERVINGS

If you're a pot roast lover like me, then your favorite family pot roast recipe is in for a challenge!

1 tablespoon vegetable oil
One 3-pound lean boneless beef
   chuck roast
1 can (14½ ounces) whole
   tomatoes, undrained, chopped
1 can (4 ounces) chopped green
   chilies

1 package (1¼ ounces) dry taco
   seasoning mix
1 beef bouillon cube, crushed
1 tablespoon light brown sugar
2 tablespoons water
1 tablespoon cornstarch

In a soup pot, heat the oil over medium heat. Add the roast and brown for 3 to 5 minutes, turning halfway through the cooking. In a small bowl, combine the tomatoes and their juice, the chilies, taco seasoning mix, bouillon, and brown sugar; mix well. Pour over the pot roast; reduce the heat to low, cover, and simmer for 3 to 3½ hours, or until the roast is fork-tender. Remove the roast to a cutting board. In a small bowl, combine the water and cornstarch. Slowly pour into the tomato mixture in the soup pot and stir over low heat until the sauce thickens. Slice the roast across the grain and serve topped with the sauce.

NOTE: If not serving this immediately, return the sliced roast to the pot with the sauce and keep warm over low heat until ready to serve.

TEXAS T-BONES

2 TO 4 SERVINGS

T-bone steaks made Texas style. . . . This sure is one meal that'll bring 'em running when they hear that dinner bell!

¼ cup olive oil
3 tablespoons ground cumin
4 garlic cloves, minced
1 teaspoon coarse (kosher) salt

½ teaspoon cayenne pepper
2 beef T-bone steaks (1 pound
    each), 1 inch thick

Preheat the broiler. In a small bowl, combine all the ingredients except the steaks; mix well. Place the steaks on a broiler pan and brush half of the seasoning mixture over the tops. Broil the steaks for 5 to 6 minutes, then remove them from the broiler, turn over, and brush with the remaining seasoning mixture. Return to the broiler and broil for 5 to 6 more minutes for medium, or to desired doneness.

NOTE: These are even better made on the grill. Prepare the steaks the same way as above, turning halfway through the grilling and brushing with the remaining seasoning mixture.

AUSTIN CHICKEN-FRIED STEAK

4 SERVINGS

What could be more Texan than a chicken-fried steak recipe that comes from the capital of Texas?

¼ cup plus 2 tablespoons all-purpose flour, divided
1½ teaspoons salt, divided
½ teaspoon cayenne pepper, divided
2¼ cups milk, divided

1 egg
½ cup dry bread crumbs
1 to 1¼ pounds beef cubed steak
1 cup vegetable oil
1 can (4 ounces) sliced black olives, drained

In a shallow dish, combine ¼ cup flour, ½ teaspoon salt, and ¼ teaspoon cayenne pepper. In another shallow dish, combine ¼ cup milk and the egg; mix well. Place the bread crumbs in a third shallow dish. Coat the steak on all sides with the flour mixture, then the egg mixture, and then the bread crumb mixture. (Discard any remaining coating mixture.) In a large deep skillet, heat the oil over medium-high heat until hot but not smoking. Add the steak and cook for 6 to 8 minutes, or until the juices run clear and the coating is golden, turning halfway through the cooking. Drain on paper towels. Pour off and discard all but 2 tablespoons of the oil remaining in the skillet. Whisk the remaining 2 tablespoons flour into the oil and brown over low heat. Add the remaining 1 teaspoon salt, ¼ teaspoon cayenne pepper, and 2 cups milk. Whisk for 3 to 4 minutes, or until thick; add the olives and stir well to mix. Place the steak on a serving platter and top with the gravy. Serve immediately.

NOTE: Be sure to add the olives just before you're ready to serve this, or they'll cook and make the gravy too salty.

 97

WAGON TRAIN POT ROAST

8 TO 10 SERVINGS

After a long hot day of driving the wagon train, there was nothing more important than a hearty meal (except maybe a good night's sleep). Times have sure changed a lot in some ways—and only a little in others. This is my way to get that old-style hearty meal. . . . The sound sleep is sure to follow!

One 4-pound beef brisket	2 large onions, thinly sliced
4 cups barbecue sauce	3 garlic cloves, minced

Preheat the oven to 350°F. Place the brisket fat side up in a large roasting pan that has been coated with nonstick vegetable spray. In a large bowl, combine the remaining ingredients; mix well and pour over the brisket. Cover tightly with aluminum foil and roast for 3 to 3½ hours, or until fork-tender. Remove the brisket to a cutting board. Trim the fat and cut the brisket across the grain into ¼-inch-thick slices. Serve topped with the sauce from the pan.

NOTE: If you want to make this in advance, return the sliced brisket to the sauce in the pan, cover, and store in the refrigerator. When ready to serve, heat the covered brisket in a 300°F. oven until warmed through.

TEXAS GOLD SIRLOIN

4 TO 6 SERVINGS

Early settlers rushed across America to pan for gold. But today you can find this "gold" right in your own kitchen pan.

One 2-pound beef top sirloin
   steak, about 1½ inches thick,
   trimmed
½ cup bourbon whiskey
¼ cup Worcestershire sauce
¼ teaspoon hot pepper sauce

1½ teaspoons dry mustard
½ teaspoon onion powder
½ teaspoon garlic powder
1 teaspoon black pepper
1 pound (4 sticks) butter

In a deep skillet, brown the steak over high heat for 4 minutes, turning halfway through the cooking. Meanwhile, in a small bowl, combine the remaining ingredients except the butter; mix well. After the steak is browned, add the butter to the skillet and reduce the heat to low. When the butter is melted, add the whiskey mixture and cook for 15 to 20 minutes, or to desired doneness, turning halfway through the cooking. Remove the steak to a cutting board and cut across the grain into thin slices. Serve immediately, topped with the sauce.

COWBOY RIBS

4 TO 6 SERVINGS

This dry seasoning rub is so good that you can use it on any type of meat, and even on chicken.

1 tablespoon ground cumin
1 tablespoon dried oregano
1 tablespoon dried thyme
1 tablespoon chili powder

1 tablespoon garlic powder
6 to 7 pounds beef baby back ribs,
   trimmed and cut into
   individual ribs

Preheat the oven to 375°F. In a small bowl, combine all the ingredients except the ribs. Line a large roasting pan with aluminum foil, then place a roasting rack on the foil. Spray the rack with nonstick vegetable spray. Rub the seasoning mixture all over the ribs, then place on the roasting rack. Roast, uncovered, for 60 to 65 minutes, or until tender.

NOTE: For some true messy barbecued rib-eatin', serve these with Texas Barbecue Sauce (page 12) on the side.

ROPA VIEJA

6 TO 8 SERVINGS

Some folks claim this as a Cuban dish, and others swear it's got Mexican origins. Either way, *ropa vieja* translates to "old clothes." Now, you might not think that that sounds too appetizing, but this traditional shredded beef dish is incredibly flavorful, and definitely worth trying.

2 tablespoons olive oil
1 large onion, chopped
1 garlic bulb, separated into
  cloves, peeled, and finely
  chopped
1 large green bell pepper, cut into
  thin strips

2 pounds beef flank steak
2 cans (15 ounces each) tomato
  sauce
2 cups dry white wine
½ teaspoon salt
½ teaspoon black pepper

In a soup pot, heat the olive oil over medium heat. Add the onion, garlic, and bell pepper and cook for 6 to 7 minutes, or until tender. Add the remaining ingredients and bring to a boil, then reduce the heat to low. Cover and simmer for 2 to 2½ hours, or until the meat is very tender, stirring occasionally. Using 2 forks, finely shred the beef. Cover and continue cooking for 10 more minutes. Serve immediately.

NOTE: This is great served over white rice. And for added color, you can add a 10-ounce package of frozen peas to the mixture for the last 10 minutes of cooking.

RANGE CHILI

6 TO 8 SERVINGS

I've been to loads of chili cook-offs, and I have to have tasted every possible type of chili . . . some with beans, others with chunky meat, or with just vegetables—and even seafood. They've all been a little different, and very tasty. But when I sampled this one recently, I decided it deserved a place among my all-time favorites.

2 pounds ground beef
½ pound chorizo sausage, diced
   (see Note)
1 medium-sized onion, chopped
1 garlic clove, minced
1 teaspoon salt
½ teaspoon black pepper

2 cans (16 ounces each) pinto
   beans, rinsed and drained
2 cans (14½ ounces each) diced
   tomatoes, undrained
1 tablespoon red wine vinegar
2 tablespoons dry chili
   seasoning mix

In a soup pot, combine the ground beef, sausage, onion, garlic, salt, and pepper over medium-high heat; cook for 6 to 8 minutes, or until no pink remains in the meat, stirring frequently. Add the remaining ingredients and bring to a boil. Reduce the heat to low and simmer for 30 minutes.

NOTE: Dish up hearty bowls of this chili topped with shredded cheese or chopped onions and serve with plenty of tortilla chips. If chorizo sausage is not available, kielbasa or any type of hot or sweet sausage can be substituted.

MEXICANA STEW

6 TO 8 SERVINGS

A little of this and a little of that make this Mexicana delicious!

3 pounds beef flank steak, cut into 1-inch cubes
½ cup all-purpose flour
¼ cup vegetable oil
2 pounds fresh mushrooms, cut in half
3 large onions, chopped
4 garlic cloves, minced

4 cans (4 ounces each) chopped green chilies, drained
1 can (15 ounces) tomato sauce
1 cup Chianti or other dry red wine
2 teaspoons salt
1 teaspoon black pepper

In a large bowl, combine the steak and flour; toss to evenly coat the steak. In a soup pot, heat the oil over medium-high heat. Add the beef and cook for 5 to 6 minutes, or until browned on all sides, stirring constantly. Add the remaining ingredients and bring to a boil. Reduce the heat to low, cover, and simmer for 2 to 2½ hours, or until the beef is fork-tender, stirring occasionally.

NOTE: Served over hot cooked rice, this makes a satisfying one-bowl meal.

RANCH MEAT LOAF

6 TO 8 SERVINGS

Whether your gang's out rustling cattle or hangin' around the homestead, this'll certainly round 'em up!

2 pounds ground beef
1 can (14½ ounces) Mexican-
   style stewed tomatoes
1 cup dry bread crumbs
1 medium-sized onion, finely
   chopped

2 eggs
1½ teaspoons ground cumin
1 teaspoon ground cloves
1 garlic clove, minced
1 teaspoon salt
½ teaspoon black pepper

Preheat the oven to 350°F. In a large bowl, combine all the ingredients; mix well. Place on a large rimmed baking sheet and form into a loaf. Bake for 70 to 75 minutes, or until the juices run clear. Drain off the excess liquid and allow to sit for 15 minutes before slicing.

NOTE: One of my favorite ways to eat meat loaf is to have it cold the day after it was made. Yup, I cut a thick slice and make a sandwich of it with white bread. Mmm!

TEX-MEX ZITI

6 TO 8 SERVINGS

I've gotta share this with you 'cause it's one of my favorite ways to combine Italian and Mexican tastes in the same casserole. And the bonus is . . . it's easy!

1 package (12 ounces) ziti
1 pound ground beef
½ a medium-sized onion, chopped
2 cups spaghetti sauce
1 cup picante sauce
1 container (15 ounces) ricotta
    cheese

2 cups (8 ounces) shredded
    Mexican cheese blend, divided
2 tablespoons chopped fresh
    cilantro or parsley

Preheat the oven to 350°F. Prepare the pasta according to the package directions. Drain, rinse, and drain again; set aside in a large bowl. Meanwhile, in a large skillet, brown the beef and onion over medium heat for 5 minutes; drain off the excess liquid. Add to the drained pasta along with the spaghetti sauce, picante sauce, ricotta cheese, and 1 cup Mexican cheese blend; stir until well combined. Spoon into a 9" × 13" baking dish that has been coated with nonstick vegetable spray and bake for 25 minutes. Remove from the oven and sprinkle with the remaining 1 cup Mexican cheese blend. Return to the oven and bake for 10 minutes, or until the cheese melts. Sprinkle with the chopped cilantro just before serving.

NOTE: For additional ethnic flavor, you might want to add a drained can of green chilies, jalapeño peppers, or black olives when you combine all of the ingredients.

PICK-A-WINNER PICADILLO

3 TO 4 SERVINGS

This sure has an interesting combination of flavors all simmered together . . . but I think it's the raisins that give it its winning taste!

2 tablespoons vegetable oil
1 pound ground beef
1 medium-sized onion, chopped
1 can (14½ ounces) whole
   tomatoes, undrained, broken up
½ cup chopped pimiento-stuffed
   olives

½ cup raisins
2 teaspoons chili powder
¼ teaspoon garlic powder
¼ teaspoon salt
¼ teaspoon black pepper

In a large skillet, heat the oil over medium heat. Add the ground beef and onion and brown the beef until no pink remains. Add the remaining ingredients and mix well. Reduce the heat to low and simmer until the mixture is hot.

NOTE: If your family doesn't love olives, just leave them out. You'll still end up with a really tasty dish.

TACO BURGERS

4 SERVINGS

No crispy taco shells to break apart, and no messy toppings to deal with. All the taste is cooked into the burgers.

1½ pounds ground beef	½ cup salsa
1 package (1¼ ounces) dry taco seasoning mix	4 hamburger buns, split

In a large bowl, combine all the ingredients except the buns and mix until thoroughly blended. Divide the mixture into 4 equal patties. Heat a large skillet over medium heat and panfry the patties for 10 to 12 minutes, or until no pink remains and the juices run clear, turning halfway through the cooking. Serve on the buns.

NOTE: If you're looking for that complete taco flavor, top each burger with a slice of (or ¼ cup shredded) Monterey Jack cheese during the last 2 minutes of cooking, then serve topped with a slice of tomato and some shredded lettuce.

MR. McILHENNY'S CHILI

4 TO 6 SERVINGS

Real Texas chili is packed with chunks of beef *and* hot pepper sauce punch, just like this one that comes from Louisiana, the home of Mr. McIlhenny and his Tabasco® sauces.

¼ cup vegetable oil

3 pounds lean beef chuck roast, well trimmed and cut into 1-inch cubes

1 medium-sized onion, chopped

3 garlic cloves, minced

3 tablespoons chili powder

2 teaspoons ground cumin

2 teaspoons salt

2 teaspoons Tabasco® pepper sauce

3 cups water

1 can (4 ounces) chopped green chilies, drained

In a large saucepan, heat the oil over medium-high heat; add the beef and cook for 5 minutes, stirring occasionally. Drain off the liquid, then add the onion and garlic and sauté for 5 minutes, or until the beef is browned on all sides and the onion is tender, stirring frequently. Stir in the chili powder, cumin, salt, and Tabasco® sauce; cook for 1 minute. Add the water and chilies and bring to a boil, stirring occasionally. Reduce the heat to low, cover, and simmer for 45 minutes. Remove the cover and simmer for 45 more minutes, or until the beef is fork-tender.

NOTE: Mr. McIlhenny suggests serving this over hot cooked rice, garnished with chopped onions, shredded cheese, and sour cream. Mmm, mmm!

LIME-PEPPER KEBABS

6 KEBABS

People everywhere love cooking their favorite foods together on a skewer, so how 'bout giving this colorful Mexican-style kebab a try?

¼ cup lime juice
¼ cup olive oil
2 tablespoons honey
2 teaspoons black pepper
1¼ pounds beef top or bottom
   round, cut into twenty-four
   1-inch cubes

6 fresh jalapeño peppers
2 frozen ears of corn on the cob,
   thawed, each cut into 6 equal-
   sized pieces (see Note)
1 large red bell pepper, cut into
   12 chunks
6 wooden or metal skewers

In a large bowl, combine the lime juice, olive oil, honey, and black pepper; mix well. Add the beef and toss to coat. Cover and chill for 4 to 6 hours, or overnight. If using wooden skewers, soak them in warm water for 20 minutes. Preheat the broiler. Thread each skewer with 1 jalapeño pepper, 2 pieces each of corn and bell pepper, and 4 pieces of beef, alternating the items evenly. Place the skewers on a baking sheet that has been coated with nonstick vegetable spray. Broil for 8 to 10 minutes for medium, or to desired doneness, turning halfway through the broiling. Serve immediately.

NOTE: You can use 2 cooked fresh ears of corn on the cob instead of frozen, if you prefer. Just cut them into 1-inch rounds. And if you'd like to grill these, go ahead. Cook them until the beef reaches desired doneness.

ORANGE-HONEY PORK RIBS

4 TO 5 SERVINGS

Sure you'll need lots of napkins, but only after you finish licking all this sweet sauce from your fingers!

4 pounds country-style pork ribs	1 teaspoon cayenne pepper sauce
1 cup orange marmalade	1 teaspoon ground cumin
½ cup honey	½ teaspoon salt

Place the ribs in a soup pot and brown for 10 to 12 minutes over medium-high heat, turning occasionally. In a medium-sized bowl, combine the remaining ingredients; mix well. Pour the mixture over the ribs, then reduce the heat to medium and continue cooking for 18 to 20 minutes, or until the rib juices run clear and no pink remains. Serve topped with the sauce.

NOTE: The marmalade and honey take care of the sweet part, but to make this a really sweet *and* spicy sauce, add more cayenne pepper sauce.

SKILLET PORK CHOPS

6 SERVINGS

Pork chops, beans, veggies, and rice. . . . Cooking it all in one skillet makes cleanup a snap. And the rich taste makes you a hero!

6 pork loin chops, 1 inch thick
(1¾ to 2 pounds total),
trimmed
½ teaspoon salt
½ teaspoon black pepper
1 tablespoon vegetable oil
2 cans (14½ ounces each) stewed
tomatoes, undrained

1 can (16 ounces) kidney beans,
rinsed and drained
1 can (15¼ ounces) whole kernel
corn, drained
⅔ cup uncooked long- or whole-
grain rice
½ cup picante sauce
1 teaspoon chili powder

Sprinkle the pork chops with the salt and pepper. Heat the oil in a large skillet over medium-high heat until hot but not smoking. Add the chops and cook for 5 to 6 minutes, or until browned, turning halfway through the cooking; remove to a platter. Add the remaining ingredients to the skillet; mix well and bring to a boil. Place the pork chops on the tomato mixture; reduce the heat to low, cover, and simmer for 20 minutes, or until the chops are cooked to medium-well or desired doneness beyond that. Remove the skillet from the heat and allow to stand, covered, for 5 minutes before serving.

NOTE: For added flavor, add a tablespoon of light brown sugar to the rice and vegetable mixture in the skillet before bringing it to a boil.

NINE-SPICE CHORIZO SAUSAGE

6 PATTIES

Chorizo is a spicy Mexican sausage, and my recipe is packed with spice . . . nine spices, to be exact!

1 pound ground pork
2 tablespoons apple cider vinegar
2 tablespoons water
1 tablespoon vegetable oil
1 garlic clove, minced
1 tablespoon paprika
1½ teaspoons chili powder

½ teaspoon dried oregano
½ teaspoon ground cinnamon
¼ teaspoon ground cloves
¼ teaspoon ground cumin
1½ teaspoons salt
½ teaspoon black pepper

In a large bowl, combine all the ingredients; mix until thoroughly combined. Cover and chill for 3 to 4 hours. Shape the mixture into 6 equal patties about 3 inches across and ½ inch thick. Heat a large nonstick skillet over medium-low heat and cook the patties for 6 to 8 minutes, or until no pink remains, turning halfway through the cooking.

NOTE: Chilling the raw meat mixture for a few hours before cooking allows it to absorb the seasonings more thoroughly, giving your finished sausage patties really rich flavor.

POULTRY/
AVES DE CORRAL

SAN ANTONIO WINGS

4 TO 6 SERVINGS

Whether you make these as a quick appetizer or a fun-to-eat main course, you're in for a treat!

1½ cups ketchup
1 cup honey
1½ cups picante sauce

5 pounds split chicken wings, thawed if frozen

In a large bowl, combine the ketchup, honey, and picante sauce. Add the chicken wings and toss to coat well. Cover and marinate in the refrigerator for 1 hour. Preheat the oven to 400°F. Remove the chicken from the marinade, reserving the marinade. Spread the wings in a single layer on two large rimmed baking sheets that have been lined with aluminum foil and coated with nonstick vegetable spray. Bake the wings for 30 minutes, then remove from the oven, turn over, and brush with the reserved marinade. **Discard any excess marinade.** Return the wings to the oven and bake for 30 more minutes, or until the chicken is crispy and no pink remains. Serve immediately.

NOTE: The spiciness of these wings depends on the intensity of the picante sauce—the hotter the sauce, the hotter the wings!

BARBECUED DRUMSTICKS

4 TO 5 SERVINGS

Barbecue is a longtime Southwestern favorite that has really caught on around the country . . . and it's easy to taste why!

10 chicken drumsticks (about 2 pounds total)	1 cup barbecue sauce
	1 teaspoon hot pepper sauce
½ teaspoon salt	2 teaspoons dried oregano
¼ teaspoon black pepper	2 teaspoons ground cumin

Preheat the oven to 375°F. Place the drumsticks in a 9" × 13" baking dish that has been coated with nonstick vegetable spray. Sprinkle with the salt and pepper, then bake for 30 minutes. In a small bowl, combine the remaining ingredients. Remove the drumsticks from the oven and pour the barbecue sauce mixture over them. Return to the oven for 30 more minutes, or until the chicken juices run clear and no pink remains.

NOTE: I like drumsticks, but any chicken parts will work here, even a whole chicken cut into 8 pieces.

SOUTHWESTERN STUFFED CHICKEN

6 SERVINGS

The secret ingredient is the spicy cheese inside each chicken breast. Sshh! Let's let it be a surprise!

1½ cups crushed cheese crackers

2 tablespoons dry taco seasoning mix

6 boneless, skinless chicken breast halves (1½ to 2 pounds total)

4 ounces Mexican-flavored processed cheese spread, cut into 6 cubes

⅓ cup butter, melted

Preheat the oven to 350°F. In a shallow bowl, combine the cracker crumbs and taco seasoning mix; set aside. With a kitchen mallet or rolling pin, gently pound the chicken to ¼-inch thickness between 2 pieces of waxed paper. Place a cube of cheese in the center of each chicken breast and roll up tightly from the short side of each breast, tucking in the sides as you roll. Brush with the melted butter, then roll in the cracker crumb mixture, holding the chicken rolls securely closed and coating on all sides. Place each rolled breast seam side down in its own cup of a 6-cup muffin tin that has been coated with nonstick vegetable spray. Bake for 25 to 30 minutes, or until no pink remains and the juices run clear. Serve immediately.

NOTE: Any type of cheese will work as a filling, including Monterey Jack–pepper cheese (if you want that extra touch of spiciness).

ROASTED CHICKEN AND ONIONS

4 TO 6 SERVINGS

I grew up on my mom's tasty roasted chicken, and today I still eat a load of chicken—mostly roasted. Well, the addition of a little chili powder and a lot of onions gives Mom's good-old roasted chicken recipe a little more competition in our kitchen these days!

One 2½- to 3-pound chicken, cut
   into 8 pieces
2 large onions, thinly sliced and
   separated into rings

1 tablespoon chili powder
1 teaspoon garlic powder
1 teaspoon onion powder
½ teaspoon salt

Preheat the oven to 350°F. In a large bowl, combine all the ingredients and toss until the chicken is thoroughly coated. Place the mixture in a 9" × 13" baking dish that has been coated with nonstick vegetable spray. Bake for 60 to 70 minutes, or until no pink remains and the juices run clear.

NOTE: If you prefer, you can roast a whole chicken rather than cutting it up. Just be sure to coat the chicken completely with the seasoning mixture and cook it for an extra 20 minutes or until no pink remains and the juices run clear.

MARGARITA CHICKEN

6 SERVINGS

Put away the blender and the tall salt-rimmed glasses, since you can't drink *this* margarita. (But you'll sure want to eat every last bite!)

1 cup Italian dressing
4 single-serving packages (about 2 ounces total) dry margarita mix
2¼ teaspoons black pepper

6 boneless, skinless chicken breast halves (1½ to 2 pounds total)
1 teaspoon cornstarch
1 lime, cut into wedges

In a large bowl, combine the dressing, margarita mix, and pepper; mix well. Add the chicken and toss to coat with the mixture. Cover and marinate in the refrigerator for 4 hours, or overnight. Preheat the broiler. Place the chicken on a broiler pan, reserving the marinade. Broil the chicken for 12 to 15 minutes, or until no pink remains and the juices run clear, turning halfway through the cooking. Remove the chicken to a platter and cover to keep warm. Pour the reserved marinade into a small saucepan and whisk in the cornstarch. Bring to a boil over medium-high heat and cook until slightly thickened. Pour the sauce over the chicken, place the lime wedges around it (for squeezing over individual servings), and serve immediately.

NOTE: This is one margarita that shouldn't be served frozen, but if you'd like, you can chill and slice the chicken, then serve it over a tossed salad for a refreshing Margarita Chicken Salad.

MOJO CHICKEN

6 SERVINGS

Mojo is a Spanish marinade that's perfect for chicken, meat, fish, or vegetables. Boy, are your taste buds in for a treat!

¾ cup grapefruit juice
¾ cup orange juice
½ cup white vinegar
1 tablespoon lemon juice
½ a medium-sized onion, chopped
2 tablespoons minced garlic

1 teaspoon ground cumin
½ teaspoon dried cilantro
2 teaspoons salt
6 boneless, skinless chicken
  breast halves (1½ to 2 pounds
  total)

In a blender, combine all the ingredients except the chicken; blend until smooth. Reserve 1 cup of the mixture; cover and chill. Place the chicken in a large glass dish and pour the remaining juice mixture over the top. Cover and marinate in the refrigerator for 2 to 3 hours. Remove the chicken from the marinade, discarding excess marinade. Heat a large skillet over medium-high heat and cook the chicken for 12 to 14 minutes, or until no pink remains and the juices run clear, turning halfway through the cooking. Meanwhile, in a small saucepan, heat the reserved 1 cup chilled marinade to boiling over medium-high heat. Pour over the cooked chicken. Serve immediately.

CASSEROLE CHICKEN POT PIE

9 TO 12 SERVINGS

Jo Ann from my kitchen staff shared this favorite family recipe with me, and I decided it was so good I had to share it with you. So, here it is!

2 cups diced cooked chicken
1 medium-sized onion, chopped
1 medium-sized red bell pepper, chopped
2 cans (4 ounces each) chopped green chilies, drained
1 can (10½ ounces) condensed cream of mushroom soup

1 can (10½ ounces) condensed cream of chicken soup
1 cup milk
12 corn tortillas
Nonstick vegetable spray
3 cups (12 ounces) shredded Mexican cheese blend

Preheat the oven to 350°F. In a large saucepan, combine the chicken, onion, bell pepper, chilies, the soups, and the milk over medium heat. Cook for 10 to 12 minutes, or until heated through, stirring occasionally. Meanwhile, spray the tortillas with nonstick vegetable spray and heat, one at a time, in a large skillet over medium heat for about 30 seconds per side. Place 6 of the heated tortillas in a single layer in the bottom of a 9" × 13" baking dish that has been coated with nonstick vegetable spray. Spoon half of the chicken mixture evenly over the tortillas and top with 1½ cups cheese. Place the remaining heated tortillas over the cheese. Top with the remaining chicken mixture and 1½ cups cheese. Bake for 30 minutes, or until thoroughly heated and the cheese is melted. Remove from the oven and allow to sit for 5 minutes before cutting and serving.

CHICKEN AND BLACK BEANS

4 SERVINGS

Look no more! Here's a stick-to-your-ribs dinner favorite that can be prepared in no time. That leaves us more time to shop in the open-air markets of Mexico . . . or our local supermarkets!

4 boneless, skinless chicken
    breast halves (1 to 1¼ pounds
    total), cut into ¾-inch strips
1 can (15 ounces) black beans,
    rinsed and drained

1 can (14½ ounces) Mexican-
    style stewed tomatoes
1½ cups water
1 cup long- or whole-grain rice
4 chicken bouillon cubes

Coat a large skillet with nonstick vegetable spray and heat over medium-high heat. Cook the chicken for 5 to 7 minutes, or until browned. Add the remaining ingredients and bring to a boil. Reduce the heat to low, cover, and simmer for 20 minutes. Remove from the heat and let stand for 5 minutes before serving.

NOTE: If you can't find Mexican-style stewed tomatoes in your supermarket, just use regular stewed tomatoes and add ¼ cup of your favorite salsa.

WAGON WHEEL PASTA AND CHICKEN

4 TO 6 SERVINGS

By starting out with wagon wheel pasta, you know you're going to have fun with this dish! Besides, it reminds us of the wagon trains that carried our ancestors West so many years ago.

1 package (12 ounces) wagon wheel pasta

4 boneless, skinless chicken breast halves (1 to 1¼ pounds total)

1 teaspoon salt, divided

¼ teaspoon black pepper

2 tablespoons olive oil

2 garlic cloves, minced

1 can (14 ounces) artichoke hearts, drained and cut in half

1 can (11 ounces) Mexican-style corn, drained

1 can (10¾ ounces) condensed cream of corn soup

1¼ cups milk

1 jar (7 ounces) roasted peppers, drained and cut into ¼-inch-wide strips

1 teaspoon hot pepper sauce

Prepare the pasta according to the package directions; drain, rinse, and drain again. Set aside in a covered dish to keep warm. Meanwhile, sprinkle the chicken with ½ teaspoon salt and the black pepper. In a large skillet, heat the oil over medium heat; add the chicken and garlic. Cook for 12 to 15 minutes, or until no pink remains in the chicken and the juices run clear, turning halfway through the cooking. Remove the chicken to a cutting board and cut into 1-inch cubes. Add the remaining ingredients to the skillet and bring to a boil over medium heat; add the chicken and cook for 3 to 5 minutes, or until thoroughly heated. Toss with the warm pasta and serve immediately.

NOTE: If you can't find wagon wheels, use rotini, elbow macaroni, or medium pasta shells.

 123

SAUCY WHITE CHILI

8 TO 10 SERVINGS

Traditional chilis had better watch out, 'cause white chili is in the picture now, and it's becoming very popular!

1 tablespoon vegetable oil
6 boneless, skinless chicken
    breast halves (1½ to 2 pounds
    total), cut into 1-inch cubes
¼ teaspoon salt
¼ teaspoon black pepper
1 medium-sized onion, chopped
1 garlic clove, minced
5 cans (16 ounces each) Great
    Northern beans, undrained

2 cans (14½ ounces each) ready-
    to-use chicken broth
1 can (14½ ounces) whole
    tomatoes, undrained,
    broken up
1 can (4 ounces) chopped green
    chilies, undrained
2 teaspoons ground cumin
1 teaspoon chili powder

In a soup pot, heat the oil over medium heat. Sprinkle the chicken with the salt and pepper and sauté for 5 to 6 minutes, until browned. Add the onion and garlic and cook for 3 to 4 minutes, or until the onion is tender. Add the remaining ingredients and bring to a boil. Reduce the heat to low and simmer, uncovered, for 50 to 60 minutes, or until the chili thickens slightly, stirring occasionally.

NOTE: For a really hearty meal, I like to serve this chili in a big bowl over hot cooked rice.

TURKEY AND BLACK BEAN CHILI

4 TO 5 SERVINGS

Make your next tailgate party a little different by offering this change-of-pace chili.

2 tablespoons vegetable oil
1 pound ground turkey breast
1 medium-sized onion, coarsely chopped
2 garlic cloves, minced
2 teaspoons chili powder
1 teaspoon ground cumin
1 teaspoon dried oregano

¼ teaspoon salt
1 can (15 ounces) black beans, rinsed and drained
1 can (14½ ounces) ready-to-use chicken broth
1 cup picante sauce
1 tablespoon cornstarch

In a large saucepan, heat the oil over medium heat. Add the turkey, onion, garlic, chili powder, cumin, oregano, and salt; cook for 8 to 10 minutes, or until the turkey is no longer pink. Stir in the beans and chicken broth. In a small bowl, combine the picante sauce and cornstarch. Add to the saucepan and bring to a boil. Reduce the heat to low and simmer, uncovered, for 10 to 12 minutes, or until thickened.

NOTE: For the leanest and healthiest Turkey and Black Bean Chili, be sure to use ground turkey *breast*, not regular ground turkey.

CORPUS CHRISTI TURKEY LOAF

4 TO 6 SERVINGS

A fan from Corpus Christi, Texas, sent me this zippy turkey loaf recipe. She says it's popular in her Southwestern city . . . and I have a feeling its popularity is about to spread!

1½ pounds ground turkey
   (see Note)
1 egg, beaten
¾ cup salsa, divided
1 can (4 ounces) chopped green
   chilies, drained

½ cup (2 ounces) shredded
   Monterey Jack cheese
½ cup dry bread crumbs
1 package (1¼ ounces) dry taco
   seasoning mix

Preheat the oven to 350°F. In a medium-sized bowl, combine all the ingredients except ¼ cup salsa; mix well. Press the mixture into a 9" × 5" loaf pan. Spread the remaining ¼ cup salsa evenly over the top and bake for 55 to 60 minutes, or until the juices run clear and no pink remains. Drain off the excess liquid. Allow to sit for 5 minutes before slicing and serving.

NOTE: Regular ground turkey creates a moister loaf than ground turkey breast (which is *very* lean), but use whichever you prefer.

MOLE (PRONOUNCED MO-LAY)

No, this isn't a mistake—I didn't forget to print the recipe for this truly Mexican dish. After doing research on *moles*, I found that it was almost impossible to make any version of it (there are many!) in the "quick and easy" Mr. Food style. First of all, there seems to be lots of disagreement on whether mole is a stew or a sauce; it's probably both, since, with a traditional mole, the sauce really *is* the dish.

There's a different version from every region of Mexico, each made with its own combination of cooked vegetables and flavorings (and dried chilies, green chilies, or tomatillos), often thickened with nuts and seeds and even touched with a bit of chocolate! You see, in order to make an authentic mole, it would take too many ingredients and too many long procedures for most of us to bother with at home—so I decided to recommend that any of us who want to experience a true mole dish go to a genuine Mexican restaurant and let them do all the work while we sit back and enjoy!

FISH AND SEAFOOD/
PESCADOS Y MARISCOS

Whew! I'm hot!

GALVESTON BAY SWORDFISH

6 SERVINGS

It might look as if it uses a lot of ingredients, but this dish comes together so quickly that before you know it, you'll be relaxing on the dock watching the sun go down.

½ cup all-purpose flour

1 teaspoon salt

½ teaspoon black pepper

2 to 2½ pounds swordfish, cut into 2-inch chunks

½ cup (1 stick) butter

1 medium-sized onion, cut into wedges

1 medium-sized green bell pepper, cut into strips

2 garlic cloves, minced

3 medium-sized ripe tomatoes, cut into wedges

½ cup dry white wine

1 can (8 ounces) tomato sauce

½ teaspoon dried oregano

In a medium-sized bowl, combine the flour, salt, and black pepper. Add the fish chunks and toss to coat completely with the flour mixture. In a large skillet, melt the butter over medium-high heat, then sauté the fish for 8 to 10 minutes, or until golden brown, turning occasionally. Add the onion, bell pepper, and garlic, and sauté for 3 to 5 minutes, or until the onion is tender. Add the remaining ingredients and cook for 6 to 8 minutes, or until thoroughly heated, stirring occasionally. Serve immediately.

NOTE: If swordfish is not available, you can use any firm, white-fleshed fish, like monkfish. For an added burst of flavor, add a drained 2¼-ounce can of sliced black olives when you add the tomatoes.

FLOUNDER VERACRUZ

4 SERVINGS

Let me introduce you to a full-tasting fish dish named for the Mexican port city of Veracruz.

½ cup (1 stick) butter, divided
1 medium-sized onion, chopped
1 medium-sized green bell pepper, chopped
1 can (14½ ounces) whole tomatoes, drained and coarsely chopped

1 jar (8 ounces) picante sauce
¼ teaspoon dried rosemary
1 to 1¼ pounds flounder fillets
1 teaspoon salt
½ teaspoon black pepper
¼ cup lime juice

In a large skillet, melt 2 tablespoons butter over medium heat. Add the onion and bell pepper and cook for 5 to 6 minutes, or until tender. Add the tomatoes, picante sauce, and rosemary and cook for 15 to 20 minutes, or until thickened. Meanwhile, sprinkle the fish with the salt and black pepper. In another large skillet, melt the remaining 6 tablespoons butter over medium heat. Add the fish and lime juice and cook for 4 to 6 minutes, or until the fish flakes easily with a fork, turning halfway through the cooking. Remove the fish to a serving platter and top with the sauce. Serve immediately.

NOTE: This dish is often served topped with capers, or chopped green olives or pimientos. And you can substitute just about any type of white-fleshed fish for the flounder if you want. Whatever is the freshest or on sale usually works for me.

CHILLED SALMON WITH AVOCADO SALSA

4 SERVINGS

I know that most people think that Tex-Mex food is all hot, hot, hot, but this recipe is just one way we can enjoy cooling it down a bit.

½ cup plus 1 teaspoon lime juice, divided

½ cup water

1 medium-sized onion, finely chopped, divided

1 garlic clove, minced

1 teaspoon dried tarragon

1 teaspoon salt, divided

1¼ to 1½ pounds salmon fillet, cut into 4 serving pieces

1 avocado, pitted, peeled, and finely chopped

1 small ripe tomato, seeded and chopped (see Note)

¼ teaspoon chili powder

In a large skillet, combine ½ cup lime juice, the water, one third of the onions, the garlic, tarragon, and ½ teaspoon salt over high heat. Bring to a boil and add the salmon. Cover and reduce the heat to medium. Poach the fish for 8 to 10 minutes, or until it flakes easily with a fork. Meanwhile, in a medium-sized bowl, combine the avocado, tomato, chili powder, and the remaining chopped onion, 1 teaspoon lime juice, and ½ teaspoon salt; mix well. Cover and chill until ready to use. Transfer the salmon and poaching liquid from the skillet to a covered dish and chill for at least 2 hours, or until ready to serve. Remove the chilled salmon from the poaching liquid and discard the liquid. Serve the salmon with the avocado salsa on the side.

NOTE: To seed a tomato, slice in half crosswise and gently squeeze out the seeds and juice.

PANFRIED RED SNAPPER

2 TO 4 SERVINGS

Recently, I was at a local Mexican restaurant where the daily special was panfried red snapper. It sounded so interesting that I had to try it, and after one bite I knew I'd made the right choice. You can, too. Give it a try!

2 whole red snapper (1 to 1½ pounds each), cleaned	1 teaspoon salt, divided
½ cup all-purpose flour	1 teaspoon black pepper, divided
	6 tablespoons butter, divided

Rinse the fish in cold water; drain but do not pat dry. In a shallow dish, combine the flour, ½ teaspoon salt, and ½ teaspoon pepper. Sprinkle the remaining ½ teaspoon each of salt and pepper inside the cavities of the fish. Completely coat the fish in the flour mixture. In each of 2 large skillets, melt 3 tablespoons butter over medium heat. Add 1 fish to each skillet and cook for 12 to 15 minutes, or until the coating is golden and the fish flakes easily with a fork, carefully turning halfway through the cooking. Serve immediately.

NOTE: If you want to cook red snapper fillets instead of the whole fish, use 1 to 1½ pounds of fillets and reduce the cooking time to 5 to 6 minutes (still turning halfway through the cooking).

MARIACHE SHRIMP

4 SERVINGS

Like a mariache singer, this shrimp is sure to bring a song to your meal.

1 pound large shrimp, peeled and deveined, with tails left on	1 tablespoon lime juice
½ cup (1 stick) butter	8 garlic cloves, minced
¼ cup vegetable oil	½ teaspoon crushed red pepper
	¼ teaspoon salt

Rinse and drain the shrimp well. In a large skillet, heat the remaining ingredients over medium-high heat. When the butter is melted, add the shrimp and cook for 2 to 3 minutes, or until the shrimp turn pink, stirring occasionally. Serve immediately.

NOTE: If you want to make it extra spicy, use additional crushed red pepper.

SHRIMP TORTILLA PIZZA

4 TO 8 SERVINGS

You won't find pepperoni and mushrooms on this pizza. It's a Mexican-style pizza, so you're in for a taste treat.

Four 10-inch flour tortillas
Nonstick vegetable spray
1 jar (16 ounces) salsa
1 package (10 ounces) frozen
  cooked shrimp, thawed and
  drained

1 can (4 ounces) sliced black
  olives, drained
2 cups (8 ounces) shredded
  Monterey Jack cheese

Preheat the oven to 350°F. Spray both sides of the tortillas lightly with nonstick vegetable spray and place on 2 large rimmed baking sheets. Bake for 10 to 12 minutes, or until crisp, turning halfway through the baking. Remove from the oven, spread with salsa, and top the tortillas evenly with the shrimp, olives, and cheese. Return to the oven and bake for 5 minutes, or until the cheese is melted. Cut each tortilla pizza into 4 wedges and serve immediately.

NOTE: Each "pizza" is a meal in itself—or you can cut them into smaller wedges and serve as an appetizer.

GULF OF MEXICO SHRIMP SCAMPI

4 SERVINGS

On the weekend after Easter, the people of Galveston, Texas, celebrate the blessing of the shrimp fleet by holding a giant seafood festival. There's usually every kind of cooked shrimp dish imaginable, including this fresh-tasting one.

1 pound large shrimp, peeled and
    deveined, with tails left on
½ cup (1 stick) butter
5 garlic cloves, minced
½ teaspoon salt

½ teaspoon cayenne pepper
3 tablespoons lime juice
1 tablespoon chopped fresh
    parsley

Rinse and drain the shrimp well. In a large skillet, melt the butter over low heat. Add the shrimp, garlic, salt, and cayenne pepper. Increase the heat to medium and cook for 2 to 3 minutes, or until the shrimp turn pink, stirring occasionally. Add the lime juice and parsley, tossing to coat, then remove from the heat and serve immediately.

NOTE: This is great served over almost any kind of pasta or rice.

ON THE SIDE/
PLATOS DE ENTRADA

YELLOW RICE

4 SERVINGS

Hmm . . . I need something to serve with my saucy Tex-Mex favorites. Oh, yeah—this rice makes a colorful addition to any meal!

1 cup long- or whole-grain white rice	1 teaspoon onion powder
2 cups water	½ teaspoon turmeric
2 teaspoons olive oil	¼ teaspoon ground cumin
	¾ teaspoon salt

In a medium-sized saucepan, combine all the ingredients and bring to a boil over high heat, stirring constantly. Reduce the heat to low, cover, and simmer for 20 minutes, or until the rice is tender and the liquid is absorbed. Remove from the heat and let sit for 5 minutes. Stir the rice and serve.

NOTE: Traditionally, saffron is used to color and flavor Mexican rice, but I don't always have it on hand and, besides, it's really expensive. So I decided to replace it with turmeric, and, you know what? It tastes just as good!

MEXI-VEGGIE RICE

4 TO 6 SERVINGS

When making rice dishes, Mexican cooks often brown raw rice before boiling or steaming it. I use that method here and, with the addition of a few colorful veggies, we've got a really exciting side dish.

2 tablespoons vegetable oil
1 cup long- or whole-grain rice
1 can (14½ ounces) diced
   tomatoes, drained
1 package (10 ounces) frozen peas
   and carrots
½ a medium-sized onion, chopped

2 fresh jalapeño peppers, stems
   and seeds removed, chopped
1 garlic clove, minced
1 can (14½ ounces) ready-to-use
   chicken broth
½ teaspoon salt
⅛ teaspoon black pepper

In a large saucepan, heat the oil over medium-high heat. Add the rice and sauté for 3 to 4 minutes, or just until golden, stirring constantly. Add the remaining ingredients and bring to a boil. Reduce the heat to low, cover, and simmer for 25 to 30 minutes, or until the rice is tender and the liquid is absorbed. Stir and serve.

NOTE: Any type of rice except instant will work here. As a matter of fact, the rice most commonly used in Mexico is what we would consider a medium-grain rice.

LONE-STAR-STATE FRIES

4 TO 6 SERVINGS

These fries are big and spicy, just like Texas, the Lone Star State.

1 tablespoon paprika
1 teaspoon chili powder
1 teaspoon salt, divided
¼ teaspoon black pepper

6 medium-sized potatoes
(about 2½ pounds), washed
2 tablespoons peanut oil

Preheat the oven to 425°F. In a large resealable plastic bag, combine the paprika, chili powder, ½ teaspoon salt, and the pepper. Seal the bag and shake to mix. Cut each potato in half, then cut each half into 4 flat wedges (see illustration). Add the peanut oil and potatoes to the seasoning in the bag, then close tightly and shake to coat well. Spread the potatoes in a single layer on a large rimmed baking sheet. Bake for 20 to 22 minutes, or until fork-tender. Sprinkle with the remaining ½ teaspoon salt and serve immediately.

NOTE: Sure, you can peel the potatoes if you want, but I like the extra crunchiness of the skin. Besides, the skin is good for us!

EASY-BAKE SCALLOPED POTATOES

9 TO 12 SERVINGS

When they plead with you to make these again, you can pretend they were time-consuming and difficult. (If they only knew how easy these are to prepare!)

10 medium-sized potatoes, peeled and thinly sliced (about 4 pounds)	1 package (2 pounds) Mexican-flavored processed cheese spread, cut into 1-inch cubes

Preheat the oven to 375°F. Place one third of the cheese cubes in the bottom of a 9" × 13" baking dish that has been coated with nonstick vegetable spray. Cover with half of the potatoes, then layer another third of the cheese cubes over the potatoes. Top with the remaining potatoes and cheese. Cover tightly with aluminum foil and bake for 60 minutes, or until the potatoes are tender and the cheese is melted. Remove the foil and return the dish to the oven for 6 to 8 minutes, or until the top is golden.

NOTE: If Mexican-flavored cheese is not available, use plain processed cheese spread and add ½ cup salsa. In that case, you may want to melt the cheese first and mix in the salsa, then toss with the potatoes and bake as directed.

MASHED YUCA

4 TO 6 SERVINGS

Never heard of yuca (except when the kids don't like something!)? It's a root vegetable with a barklike outer skin. When it's peeled and boiled, it makes a unique-tasting side dish that sure gives mashed potatoes a run for their money!

3½ to 4 pounds fresh yuca, peeled
   and cut lengthwise in half
1½ teaspoons salt, divided
½ cup milk

½ cup (1 stick) butter
½ teaspoon chili powder
½ teaspoon black pepper

Cut the inner core out of the yuca and discard. Cut the yuca into thin half-circles and place in a soup pot. Add just enough water to cover the yuca completely. Add 1 teaspoon salt and bring to a boil

over medium-high heat. Cook for 30 to 40 minutes, or until fork-tender. Drain thoroughly and place in a large bowl. Add the remaining ingredients, including the remaining ½ teaspoon salt, and mash with a potato masher or fork until well combined. Serve immediately.

NOTE: Yuca can usually be found in the produce department of your supermarket near the potatoes or with the exotic fruits and vegetables.

CORN BREAD PUDDING

6 TO 9 SERVINGS

A bit different from traditional corn bread, this is rich and spoon-able—with a hint of sweetness.

1 can (15 ounces) cream-style
  corn
2 cups self-rising cornmeal

2 cups heavy cream
⅓ cup sugar
¼ cup (½ stick) butter, melted

Preheat the oven to 350°F. In a medium-sized bowl, combine all the ingredients and stir until well blended. Pour the mixture into an 8-inch square baking dish that has been coated with nonstick vegetable spray. Bake for 45 to 50 minutes, or until golden around the edges.

NOTE: Since this is sweeter and looser than traditional corn bread, I use an ice cream scoop to serve it.

SOUTHWESTERN VEGETABLE MEDLEY

4 TO 6 SERVINGS

If vegetables looked and tasted this good all the time, no one would have a problem getting their recommended five daily servings!

¼ cup vegetable oil
1 teaspoon garlic powder
¼ teaspoon cayenne pepper
1 teaspoon salt
2 medium-sized zucchini, cut into
　½-inch chunks
3 medium-sized yellow squash,
　cut into ½-inch chunks

2 large red bell peppers, cut into
　¼-inch strips
3 frozen ears of corn on the cob,
　thawed and sliced into ½-inch
　circles
3 fresh jalapeño peppers, stems
　and seeds removed, sliced into
　rings

In a small bowl, combine the oil, garlic powder, cayenne pepper, and salt; mix well. Place in a large skillet and heat over medium-high heat. Add the zucchini, yellow squash, and bell peppers; cook for 6 to 8 minutes, or until the vegetables are tender, stirring occasionally. Add the corn and jalapeños; mix well. Cook for 5 to 6 minutes, or until thoroughly heated. Serve immediately.

NOTE: As usual, it's your call . . . use these or other vegetables according to your likes and dislikes.

SIMPLE RED BEANS

4 TO 6 SERVINGS

Bingo! You found the perfect easy side dish to complete your Mexican meal . . . with just four ingredients!

2 tablespoons olive oil
1 medium-sized onion, chopped

2 cans (15 ounces each) kidney beans, undrained, divided
1 teaspoon ground cumin

In a medium-sized saucepan, heat the olive oil over medium heat; sauté the onion for 3 to 5 minutes, or until tender. Add 1½ cans of beans and the cumin. Pour the remaining ½ can of beans into a small bowl and mash with a spoon; add to the saucepan and mix well. Cook over medium heat for 5 to 8 minutes, or until thoroughly heated.

NOTE: Serve these beans with white rice for your own easy version of red beans and rice.

REFRIED BEANS

4 TO 6 SERVINGS

Traditionally, refried beans take hours of soaking, cooking, and mashing. Now, in under 10 minutes, you can be enjoying your own homemade refried beans!

½ cup vegetable oil
1 medium-sized onion, chopped
2 garlic cloves, minced

3 cans (16 ounces each) pinto
    beans, rinsed and drained
½ teaspoon salt

In a large skillet, heat the oil over medium heat. Add the onion and garlic and sauté for 5 to 6 minutes, or until the onion is tender. Add the beans and salt, and mash gently with a potato masher or fork until thoroughly mashed. Continue cooking for 3 to 4 more minutes, or until heated through, stirring frequently. Serve immediately.

NOTE: These are great by themselves, but you can also use them in place of the ground beef filling in Muy Bueno Tacos (page 76) if you want to make vegetarian tacos.

HOMESTYLE BLACK BEANS

4 TO 6 SERVINGS

I bet if early Southwesterners had had indoor stoves and canned beans, they'd have loved them for making this favorite dish that used to be simmered for hours over the fire.

3 tablespoons olive oil
1 large green bell pepper, finely
    chopped
6 garlic cloves, minced
2 cans (15 ounces each) black
    beans, undrained

1 cup water
2 tablespoons red wine vinegar
3 bay leaves

In a medium-sized saucepan, heat the oil over medium-high heat; sauté the pepper and garlic for 8 to 10 minutes, or until the pepper is tender. Add the remaining ingredients; reduce the heat to medium-low and simmer, uncovered, for 30 minutes. **Be sure to remove the bay leaves before serving.** Serve immediately.

NOTE: These are typically served over white or yellow rice.

GOLDEN FRIED PLANTAINS

4 TO 6 SERVINGS

How can something so good be so easy? See for yourself. And you'd better make a lot of these, 'cause they disappear as soon as they're ready.

About ½ cup (1 stick) butter

4 very ripe plantains (see Note), peeled and cut into ¼-inch diagonal slices

In a large skillet, heat 2 tablespoons butter over medium heat. Place a single layer of plantain slices in the skillet and sauté for 6 to 8 minutes, or until golden brown, turning halfway through the cooking. Remove from the skillet and drain on paper towels. Repeat with the remaining plantains, adding butter as needed. Serve immediately.

NOTE: Plaintains are sold in varying stages of ripeness—anywhere from green to black. To ripen them, store in a paper bag in a warm, dark place until ready. The skin should be completely black before you use them in this recipe.

SWEET-AND-SPICY PICKLES

ABOUT 8 CUPS

No canning jars needed here! And there are no weeks of waiting, either. This is a perfect way to use your abundance of cucumbers, and you can sink your teeth into these homemade pickles in a jiffy.

4 cups white vinegar
4 cups sugar
1 tablespoon pickling spice

1 fresh jalapeño pepper, stem and
    seeds removed
2 pounds cucumbers, sliced
    ⅛ inch thick

In a large saucepan, combine the vinegar, sugar, pickling spice, and jalapeño over high heat. Bring to a boil and add the cucumber slices; return to a boil and cook for 15 minutes, stirring occasionally. Remove from the heat and allow to cool for 15 to 20 minutes, or until lukewarm. Place in an airtight glass or plastic container and chill until ready to serve.

NOTE: I like to use small Kirby cucumbers, but any type of cucumbers work here. Oh—for really crisp pickles, instead of cooking the cucumbers, just pour the boiling-hot pickling mixture over the cucumber slices in a large heat-proof bowl. Allow to cool slightly, then cover and chill overnight. These should keep for up to 1 month.

BEVERAGES/
BEBIDAS

155

FROZEN VIRGIN MARGARITAS

4 SERVINGS

After a siesta, wake up your taste buds with this nonalcoholic version of a true Mexican classic.

½ cup lime juice
½ cup orange juice
⅓ cup lemon juice

¾ cup sugar, divided
4 cups ice cubes, divided

In a blender, combine the lime juice, orange juice, lemon juice, ½ cup sugar, and 2 cups ice cubes. Blend for 15 to 20 seconds on high speed, or until the ice is crushed. Add the remaining ice cubes and blend for 15 to 20 more seconds, until slushy. Place the remaining ¼ cup sugar in a shallow bowl. Dip the rim of each glass into the margarita mixture, then into the sugar until the rim is coated. Fill the glasses with the margarita mixture and serve immediately.

NOTE: To make these even more fun, serve them with colorful straws. And if you'd rather be more traditional, dip the glass rims in salt instead of sugar, and garnish each with a wedge of lime.

FIVE-AND-TEN LIMEADE

6 TO 8 SERVINGS

With five cups of water and the juice of ten limes, you can see why I call this five-and-ten limeade. Plus, it reminds me of the drink I used to get at the five-and-dime store in downtown Troy, New York, where I grew up.

5 cups water
Juice of 10 limes

1 cup sugar
4 cups ice cubes

In a large pitcher, combine the water, lime juice, and sugar; stir well. Add the ice and serve immediately.

NOTE: Pour each serving into a tall glass, add a straw, and garnish with a slice of lime for that "fresh from the tree" flavor.

FROZEN LIME COOLER

4 SERVINGS

Whether you're rounding up some friends or spending a lazy summer afternoon at home, this is the easy answer to quenching that thirst.

1 pint lime sherbet   2 tablespoons lime juice
2 cups low-fat milk   2 tablespoons sugar

Combine all the ingredients in a blender and blend until thoroughly mixed. Serve immediately.

NOTE: Serve each with a wedge of lime and a dollop of whipped cream, if desired.

PEDRO'S SANGRÍA

8 TO 10 SERVINGS

Don't let this sangría fool you—it tastes fruity and really refreshing, yet it packs a powerful punch. Oh—this one's for adults only. Sorry, kids!

1 container (6 ounces) frozen limeade concentrate, thawed
1 container (6 ounces) frozen lemonade concentrate, thawed
1 container (6 ounces) frozen cranberry juice cocktail concentrate, thawed
4 cups Burgundy or other dry red wine

2 cups cold water
16 maraschino cherries
1 lime, washed and thinly sliced
1 orange, washed and thinly sliced
Ice cubes

In a large pitcher, combine the limeade, lemonade, and cranberry concentrates; add the wine and water and stir until well combined. Stir in the remaining ingredients except the ice and serve immediately in ice-filled tall glasses or wine glasses.

NOTE: If you're not serving this immediately, don't add the cherries and the sliced lime and orange; wait until you're ready to serve it.

JALAPEÑO MARTINI SPRITZER

8 SERVINGS

When planning the fiesta menu, don't forget the drinks. With each sip, you're gonna get the zing of the jalapeño pepper and the "ahh" of the spritzer.

2 fresh jalapeño peppers, cut in
   half lengthwise and seeded
1 cup gin

Ice cubes
1 liter club soda (about 4 cups)

Cut each jalapeño half in half again and place in a pitcher or clean small jar; add the gin. Cover and chill for 8 hours, or overnight. Remove the jalapeño peppers from the gin and reserve. Pour 1 ounce of the gin into each of 8 ice-filled tall glasses. Top each with about ½ cup club soda and garnish with the jalapeño pepper slices, if desired.

NOTE: Remember: This drink is for adults only . . . ones who AREN'T going to drive!

CLASSIC MARGARITA

4 SERVINGS

Make a single batch when it's just a few of you, but make several batches if you're going to fill a punch bowl for a crowd (of adults only, of course).

Coarse salt for rims of glasses
1 lime, cut into wedges
¾ cup tequila

½ cup Triple Sec
¼ cup lime juice
Ice cubes

Place the salt in a shallow dish. Run a lime wedge around the rim of 4 wine or martini glasses, then dip the rims of the glasses into the salt, coating the rims completely. Place the tequila, Triple Sec, and lime juice in a pitcher filled with ice. Stir until the mixture is cold, and pour into the salted glasses. Garnish each glass with a lime wedge.

NOTE: To serve over ice or not to serve over ice, that is the question. The answer is up to you; either way is correct.

TEQUILA SUNRISE

4 SERVINGS

Shades of yellow, orange, and red light up the sky as the sun rises. And now the adults in your group can enjoy those same colors without getting up before dawn!

Ice cubes
2 cups orange juice
¾ cup tequila

4 teaspoons grenadine syrup or
   maraschino cherry juice
¼ cup club soda (optional)
1 lime, cut into wedges

Fill 4 tall glasses half-full with ice. Pour the orange juice and tequila into a pitcher filled with ice; mix well. Pour into the glasses, then spoon 1 teaspoon grenadine syrup into each glass and allow it to sink to the bottom. Add a splash of club soda to each glass, if desired, then squeeze 1 lime wedge into each drink. Serve immediately.

NOTE: Serve with straws so that each guest can stir his or her own "sunrise."

COFFEE MILK SHAKE

3 TO 4 SERVINGS

Mexico is a large producer of coffee-flavored liqueur, so it was only natural to add it to our milk shakes to give them a whole new dimension!

1 quart coffee ice cream
¾ cup milk
¼ cup coffee-flavored liqueur

2 tablespoons chocolate-flavor
  syrup

Combine all the ingredients in a blender and, on high speed, pulse for 1 minute, or until well blended. Pour into tall glasses and serve immediately.

NOTE: A quarter cup of strong black coffee can be substituted for the coffee-flavored liqueur when you want a nonalcoholic version of this yummy treat.

MEXICAN HOT CHOCOLATE

8 SERVINGS

Mexican chocolate is rich and flavorful, and it's easy to have those same flavors in our own homemade hot chocolate. When we combine plain cocoa with these spices . . . boy, is it warm and inviting!

1½ cups cold water
½ cup sugar
⅓ cup unsweetened cocoa
2 tablespoons all-purpose flour

1 teaspoon ground cinnamon
¼ teaspoon ground cloves
6 cups milk
1 tablespoon vanilla extract

In a large saucepan, combine the water, sugar, cocoa, flour, cinnamon, and cloves. Heat over medium heat for 3 to 5 minutes, or until the sugar and cocoa are dissolved and the mixture is thoroughly combined, stirring constantly. Add the milk and heat, but do not allow to boil. Remove from the heat and stir in the vanilla; serve immediately.

NOTE: For extra creaminess, top each mug with whipped cream. Oh, yes—don't forget to dust each serving with a bit of cocoa and maybe even some slivered almonds.

MEXICAN COFFEE

4 SERVINGS

Many fancy restaurants now offer coffee flavored with liqueurs and cordials . . . for up to four or five times the cost of a cup of regular coffee! Now you can make your own at home for a lot less.

4 cups brewed coffee
½ cup coffee-flavored liqueur

½ cup whipped cream or thawed
   frozen whipped topping
Ground cinnamon for garnish

Pour the coffee into 4 mugs or coffee cups, filling them three-quarters full. Stir 2 tablespoons coffee liqueur into each cup. Top each with a dollop of whipped cream and a sprinkle of cinnamon. Serve immediately.

NOTE: For a mocha Mexican coffee, stir in 1 tablespoon chocolate-flavor syrup along with the coffee-flavored liqueur. Mmm!

DESSERTS/
POSTRES

LIME MARGARITA BARS

20 TO 24 BARS

Traditional margaritas are made in glasses with salted rims. These cooling bars are made with salted pretzels, so you get that salty taste in every bite. (And you don't sip these, so you don't need straws!)

2 cups finely crushed pretzels
¼ cup sugar
½ cup (1 stick) butter, melted
2 cans (14 ounces each)
   sweetened condensed milk

3 eggs, lightly beaten
½ cup lime juice
4 teaspoons grated lime peel

Preheat the oven to 350°F. Line a 9" × 13" baking dish with aluminum foil, allowing the foil to hang over the sides; coat the foil with nonstick baking spray. In a medium-sized bowl, combine the pretzels, sugar, and butter. Press the mixture firmly over the bottom of the prepared pan. Bake for 8 to 10 minutes, or until the crust is firm. Remove from the oven and cool slightly, leaving the oven on. Meanwhile, in a large bowl, combine the remaining ingredients. Pour into the cooled crust. Bake for 25 to 30 minutes, or until the center is firm. Cool completely on a wire rack. Pull up the ends of the foil to remove from the pan, and cut into bars.

NOTE: These freeze well, but be sure to place them in a tightly covered container. To serve, just remove as many as needed and thaw at room temperature for about 30 minutes.

ADOBE BARS

20 TO 24 BARS

Lots of rich dessert recipes are so fancy and have so many complicated steps that by the time you finish making them, you're exhausted. That's not *my* kind of dessert, and here's the proof—an easy, hearty, comforting dessert that won *everybody's* raves in my offices and test kitchen!

½ cup (1 stick) butter, softened
1 cup granulated sugar
1 whole egg
2 eggs, separated
1½ cups all-purpose flour
1 teaspoon baking powder

¼ teaspoon salt
1 cup chopped walnuts
1 cup miniature marshmallows
½ cup semisweet chocolate chips
1 cup firmly packed light brown
    sugar

Preheat the oven to 350°F. In a medium-sized bowl, with an electric beater on medium speed, cream the butter and granulated sugar. Add the whole egg and the 2 egg yolks; beat until well mixed. Add the flour, baking powder, and salt; mix well. Spread into a 9" × 13" baking dish that has been coated with nonstick baking spray. Sprinkle with the nuts, marshmallows, and chocolate chips. In a medium-sized bowl, with an electric beater on medium speed, beat the egg whites until stiff peaks form, then fold in the brown sugar. Spread over the top of the batter and bake for 30 to 35 minutes, or until golden brown. Remove from the oven and allow to cool, then cut into bars and serve.

NOTE: No miniature marshmallows on hand? Just cut regular-sized marshmallows into 6 pieces each.

BUÑUELOS

10 SERVINGS

If you think that flour tortillas are only good for making fajitas and soft tacos, think again . . . while you're enjoying this crispy sweet treat!

⅓ cup sugar
2 teaspoons ground cinnamon
Vegetable oil for frying
Ten 6-inch flour tortillas, cut into
    quarters

⅓ cup honey
⅓ cup chopped walnuts

In a small bowl, combine the sugar and cinnamon; mix well. In a large skillet, heat ¼ inch oil over medium heat until hot but not smoking (or heat to 375°F. in an electric skillet). Add several tortilla quarters and fry for 30 to 40 seconds, or until crisp and golden brown, turning halfway through the frying. Drain on paper towels and, while still warm, sprinkle with the sugar mixture. Fry the remaining tortillas and sprinkle with the sugar mixture. Drizzle with the honey and sprinkle with the chopped walnuts. Serve immediately.

NOTE: For an out-of-this-world sundae, place several sugared quarters on a plate, top with a scoop of vanilla ice cream, then drizzle with the honey and sprinkle with the walnuts.

CHOCOLATE MEXICAN WEDDING COOKIE CAKE

1 CAKE (ABOUT 4 DOZEN COOKIE BALLS)

I'd like to see someone try to set a bride and groom cake center-piece on top of *this* cake! No go—'cause it's actually made with individual cookie balls piled into a pyramid to create one big cake. I've never seen this served at a wedding, but I guess you just take as many cookie balls off the cake as you want, instead of really "cutting" the cake. However it's served, it has to be fun . . . and you know that the first bite is always filled with love, best wishes, and a lifetime of "OOH IT'S SO GOOD!!"

¾ cup (1½ sticks) butter, softened
¾ cup firmly packed light brown
   sugar
3 squares (1 ounce each)
   unsweetened baking chocolate,
   melted

1 teaspoon vanilla extract
2 cups all-purpose flour
1 cup finely chopped walnuts
½ teaspoon salt
⅔ cup confectioners' sugar

Preheat the oven to 350°F. In a large bowl, with an electric beater on medium speed, cream the butter and brown sugar until light and fluffy. Add the chocolate and vanilla and beat until well combined. Add the remaining ingredients except the confectioners' sugar and stir with a spoon until the dough is well mixed and smooth. With your hands, shape heaping teaspoonfuls of the dough into 1-inch balls and place 1 inch apart on ungreased baking sheets. Bake for 8 to 10 minutes, or until set. Remove from the oven and cool on the baking sheets for 5 minutes. Place the confectioners' sugar in a small bowl. While the chocolate balls are still warm, roll them in the sugar until completely coated. When completely cooled, roll in

172

the sugar again, then mound on a large serving platter in a pyramid shape. Cover tightly with plastic wrap and store at room temperature.

NOTE: Give this the "finishing touch" by dusting it with additional confectioners' sugar just before serving.

TEXAS HALF-MOONS

ABOUT 3 DOZEN

I've heard that werewolves come out during a full moon. Well, just you watch the cookie lovers come out for these half-moons!

1 cup (2 sticks) butter, softened	3 cups all-purpose flour
¾ cup sugar	1 tablespoon plus 2 teaspoons
1 egg	ground ginger, divided
½ cup molasses	1½ teaspoons baking soda
½ cup hot water	1 teaspoon ground cinnamon
1 teaspoon vanilla extract	1 can (16 ounces) vanilla frosting

Preheat the oven to 350°F. In a medium-sized bowl, with an electric beater on high speed, beat the butter and sugar for 2 to 3 minutes, or until fluffy. Add the egg and beat for 1 to 2 minutes, or until creamy. Beat in the molasses, water, and vanilla. Slowly add the flour, 1 tablespoon ginger, the baking soda, and cinnamon, beating for 2 to 3 minutes, until well blended. Spoon the batter by heaping tablespoonfuls 2 inches apart onto cookie sheets that have been coated with nonstick baking spray. Bake for 8 to 9 minutes, or until the edges are golden. Remove from the oven and cool on a wire rack. In a small bowl, combine the frosting and the remaining 2 teaspoons ginger. Frost half of each cookie top with about 1 tablespoon frosting.

NOTE: Of course, if your gang prefers full moons (and really likes frosting), these can become full moons if you frost the cookie tops completely.

CHOCOLATE DROPS

ABOUT 3 DOZEN

After a long hard day, you deserve to take off your cowboy boots (or whatever!) and sit down with some ice-cold milk and a few chocolate drop cookies. Come on, treat yourself!

1½ cups (3 sticks) butter, softened
1¾ cups confectioners' sugar, divided
1 egg

1 teaspoon vanilla extract
⅓ cup unsweetened cocoa
¼ teaspoon ground cinnamon
2½ cups all-purpose flour

Preheat the oven to 375°F. In a large bowl, with an electric beater on medium speed, beat the butter, 1½ cups confectioners' sugar, the egg, vanilla, cocoa, and cinnamon until well blended. Slowly add the flour and continue beating until well combined. Drop by heaping teaspoonfuls 2 to 3 inches apart onto ungreased baking sheets. Bake for 7 to 8 minutes, or until set. Remove from the baking sheets to wire racks and allow to cool completely. When cooled, lightly sprinkle with the remaining ¼ cup confectioners' sugar, and store in an airtight container until ready to serve.

NOTE: For a crisper cookie that's more like a biscuit, make these drops a little smaller and flatten them a bit with the palm of your hand before baking.

SOPAIPILLAS

ABOUT 4 DOZEN

South of the border they call these fried pastry squares *sopaipillas*. In my kitchen, my grandchildren call them their favorite crunchy after-school snack!

2¼ cups all-purpose flour, divided
2 tablespoons vegetable
   shortening
2 teaspoons baking powder

1 teaspoon salt
⅔ cup lukewarm water
Vegetable oil for deep-frying
½ cup honey

In a medium-sized bowl, combine 2 cups flour, the shortening, baking powder, and salt; mix with a spoon until crumbly. Slowly add the water and stir until the mixture comes away from the sides of the bowl. Cover and chill for 30 minutes. Sprinkle a large cutting board with the remaining ¼ cup flour and roll the dough out to ⅛-inch thickness. Cut into 2-inch squares. In a large soup pot or a deep-fryer, heat 1 inch of oil over medium-high heat until hot but not smoking. Fry the dough squares in the hot oil for 3 to 4 minutes, or until the dough is puffy and golden, turning halfway through the cooking. **Be careful: The oil is very hot.** Drain on paper towels, then stack on a plate and drizzle with the honey.

QUICK TRES LECHES

12 TO 15 SERVINGS

Tres leches translates as "three milks." Quick Tres Leches translates to a moist, decadent dessert that's prepared in minutes (and gone just as quickly)!

2 cups (1 pint) heavy cream, divided
1 can (14 ounces) sweetened condensed milk, divided

One 10-ounce prepared angel food cake, cut into ½-inch slices
1 can (5 ounces) evaporated milk

In a medium-sized bowl, with an electric beater on medium speed, beat 1½ cups heavy cream until stiff peaks form. Add 3 tablespoons sweetened condensed milk; stir to mix well. Cover and chill for about 10 minutes. Place the cake slices in a 9" × 13" baking dish. In a medium-sized bowl, whisk together the evaporated milk and the remaining sweetened condensed milk and ½ cup cream. Pour over the cake slices and cover; allow to sit for about 15 minutes. Top the cake with the chilled whipped cream mixture and serve immediately, or chill until ready to serve.

NOTE: You can usually find prepared angel food cakes in the bakery department of your supermarket. Of course, if you have the time, go ahead and make your own.

BANANAS 'N' CREAM SQUARES

12 TO 15 SERVINGS

Wow! If you're a banana lover like I am, you just stumbled across a dream-come-true dessert!

½ cup (1 stick) chilled butter
1 cup *self-rising* flour (*not* all-purpose flour)
1 cup chopped pecans, divided
1 package (8 ounces) cream cheese, softened
1 cup confectioners' sugar

1 container (12 ounces) frozen whipped topping, thawed, divided
4 ripe bananas
2 packages (4-serving size) banana or vanilla instant pudding and pie filling
3 cups milk

Preheat the oven to 350°F. In a large bowl, cut the butter into the flour and mix with a fork until the mixture is crumbly. Add ½ cup pecans and mix well. Press the mixture over the bottom of a 9" × 13" baking dish that has been coated with nonstick baking spray. Bake for 15 to 20 minutes, or until light golden. Remove from the oven and allow to cool. In a large bowl, with an electric beater on medium speed, beat the cream cheese and confectioners' sugar until well combined. Add half the whipped topping; mix well. Pour over the cooled crust. Cut the bananas into ¼-inch slices and arrange in a single layer over the cream cheese layer. In a large bowl, with an electric beater on medium speed, beat the pudding mix and milk until creamy. Spoon over the bananas and top with the remaining whipped topping. Sprinkle with the remaining ½ cup chopped pecans. Cover and chill for at least 1 hour before serving.

NOTE: If you prefer, garnish these with confectioners' sugar instead of topping them with honey. Just put ½ cup confectioners' sugar into a resealable plastic storage bag, add the cooled fried dough squares, close, and shake until the squares are completely covered.

MOCHA MOUSSE

6 TO 8 SERVINGS

Three ingredients and you're on your way to a south-of-the-border favorite. Watch—it's gonna be a favorite in the north, east, and west, too!

1 cup (6 ounces) semisweet
   chocolate chips

2 cups (1 pint) heavy cream
¼ cup coffee-flavored liqueur

In a small saucepan, melt the chocolate over low heat, stirring constantly until smooth. Set aside until slightly cooled. In a large bowl, with an electric beater on medium speed, beat the cream until stiff peaks form. Gently fold in the melted chocolate, then gently fold in the coffee-flavored liqueur. Cover and chill until ready to serve.

NOTE: For good ol' mocha mousse without the alcohol, substitute ⅛ teaspoon instant coffee granules dissolved in 1 teaspoon warm water for the coffee-flavored liqueur.

CHOCOLATE TRES LECHES

12 TO 15 SERVINGS

STOP! If you plan on making just one dessert from this book, this has *got* to be it!

1 cup all-purpose flour
¼ cup plus 2 teaspoons
    unsweetened cocoa, divided
1 teaspoon baking powder
½ teaspoon salt
5 eggs
1 cup sugar

⅓ cup water
1 tablespoon vanilla extract
1 can (12 ounces) evaporated
    milk
1 can (14 ounces) sweetened
    condensed milk
1 cup (½ pint) heavy cream

Preheat the oven to 400°F. In a medium-sized bowl, combine the flour, ¼ cup cocoa, the baking powder, and salt; set aside. In a large bowl, with an electric beater on high speed, beat the eggs and sugar on high speed for 2 to 3 minutes, or until creamy. Add the water and vanilla and beat for 8 to 10 minutes, or until doubled in volume. Fold in the flour mixture and pour into a 9" × 13" baking dish that has been coated with nonstick baking spray. Bake for 20 to 25 minutes, or until a wooden toothpick inserted in the center comes out clean. Remove from the oven and allow to cool on a wire rack. While the cake is cooling, in a medium-sized bowl, whisk together the evaporated and condensed milks, the cream, and the remaining 2 teaspoons cocoa. With a fork or a knife, poke holes over the entire top of the cake. Pour the milk mixture over the cake and allow it to be absorbed. Cover and chill for at least 2 hours before serving.

NOTE: I like to serve each piece of this on a bed of Mocha Mousse (opposite page) and top it off with a dollop of mousse. Boy, is that a chocolate lover's delight!

181

SPANISH FLAN

12 TO 14 SERVINGS

No Tex-Mex book would be complete without a flan recipe. Originated by the Spanish way before my time, creamy, custardy flan is enjoyed by all today!

1½ cups sugar, divided
8 eggs

2 teaspoons vanilla extract
4 cups whole milk

Preheat the oven to 350°F. In a small saucepan, cook ½ cup sugar over medium heat until completely melted, golden, and caramelized, stirring occasionally. Immediately pour into a 6-cup tube pan,

coating the bottom of the pan. **Be careful when working with caramelized sugar: It is very hot!** In a large bowl, with an electric beater on medium speed, beat the eggs and vanilla for 1 minute. Add the remaining 1 cup sugar and beat until well combined. Add the milk and beat until completely mixed. Pour over the caramelized sugar in the tube pan. Place the tube pan in a large baking pan of hot water, with just enough water to go halfway up the sides of the tube pan. Bake for 65 to 70 minutes, or until a knife inserted in the center comes out clean. Carefully remove from the hot water bath and allow to cool for 20 minutes. Cover and chill for at least 3 hours, or overnight. Just before serving, run a knife around the edge of the pan to loosen the flan from the pan. Carefully invert the flan onto a 12-inch *rimmed* serving plate (so that the caramel sauce doesn't run off the plate). Serve each wedge with some of the caramel sauce.

NOTE: This is one recipe that's definitely better when made the night before, so that the flan is thoroughly chilled before serving.

NOT-FRIED "FRIED" ICE CREAM

8 SERVINGS

If you've ever had fried ice cream in a Mexican restaurant, you've probably wished you knew how to make it at home. Yes, they really do deep-fry it—and that can be a pain. Well, I've got an easy short-cut way to create the same taste without all the work. It's super for last-minute company.

1 quart vanilla ice cream
2½ cups oven-toasted corn cereal, coarsely crushed

1 tablespoon butter, melted
2 tablespoons sugar
1 teaspoon ground cinnamon

Preheat the oven to 350°F. With a large spoon or an ice cream scoop, form 8 ice cream balls, each about 2½ inches in diameter, and place on a rimmed cookie sheet that has been lined with waxed paper; place in the freezer for about 1 hour. Meanwhile, in a medium-sized bowl, combine the remaining ingredients; mix well and spread on a large rimmed baking sheet that has been coated with nonstick vegetable spray. Bake for 5 to 7 minutes, or until lightly browned and crisp. Remove to a shallow dish and allow to cool completely. Remove the ice cream balls from the freezer and roll in the cereal mixture, coating on all sides. Place on a rimmed baking sheet that has been lined with clean waxed paper and freeze for 2 to 3 hours, or until the ice cream is firm; serve immediately, or cover until ready to serve.

NOTE: For a real treat, serve each "ball" in a sundae glass, drizzled with honey.

ICE CREAM BANANA ROLL-UPS

6 SERVINGS

Keep a few of these roll-ups in your freezer for when company drops by. All you'll have to do is whip up the caramelized banana sauce (it takes under 10 minutes!) to really impress your guests!

1 quart vanilla ice cream
Six 6-inch flour tortillas
½ cup (1 stick) butter
½ cup firmly packed light brown
   sugar

¼ teaspoon ground cinnamon
¼ cup coffee-flavored liqueur
3 ripe bananas, cut into ¼-inch
   slices

Place a large scoop of ice cream toward one edge of each tortilla and roll up crepe-style. Place seam side down on a rimmed cookie sheet, then cover and freeze until ready to use. In a large skillet, combine the butter, brown sugar, and cinnamon over medium heat and cook for 2 to 3 minutes, or until the butter melts and the mixture begins to caramelize, stirring frequently. Stir in the coffee liqueur and bananas and cook for 3 to 4 minutes, or until the mixture is warmed through. Remove the ice cream–filled tortillas from the freezer, place on dessert plates, and spoon the banana sauce evenly over the tops. Serve immediately.

NOTE: The tortillas can be filled with the ice cream and kept frozen for up to a week as long as they're well covered.

TEXAS STICKY BUNS

8 BUNS

A mug of hot chocolate, a Sunday newspaper, and some Texas sticky buns. . . . Oh, what a perfect Sunday morning!

4 tablespoons (½ stick) butter, divided
1 tablespoon light corn syrup
½ cup firmly packed light brown sugar, divided

½ cup pecan halves
1 package (10 ounces) refrigerated pizza crust (see Note)
2 teaspoons ground cinnamon

Preheat the oven to 350°F. In a small saucepan, combine 3 tablespoons butter, the corn syrup, and ¼ cup brown sugar over low heat, stirring constantly until the butter is melted. Immediately pour into the bottom of an 8- or 9-inch round cake pan, tilting the pan to completely cover the bottom. Immediately arrange the pecan halves flat side up in the syrup. Melt the remaining 1 tablespoon butter in the saucepan. Unroll the pizza dough on a floured surface and brush with the butter. Sprinkle with the remaining ¼ cup brown sugar and the cinnamon. Starting at a wide end, roll the dough up jelly-roll style. With a sharp knife, cut into 8 equal slices. Arrange the slices cut side up in the cake pan. Bake for 20 to 22 minutes, or until golden. Remove from the oven and immediately invert onto a serving platter. **Be careful: The caramel is very hot.** Allow to cool slightly, then serve warm.

NOTE: Refrigerated pizza crust comes in a tube and can usually be found in the dairy section of your supermarket near the refrigerated biscuits.

SPICY PECAN BRITTLE

ABOUT 1 POUND

I need your opinion—some folks in my test kitchen thought that this brittle was more spicy than sweet, while others thought it was more sweet than spicy. You know, it's funny—no matter which camp they were in, they couldn't stop eating it!

¾ cup (1½ sticks) butter
¼ cup light corn syrup
1 cup firmly packed light brown
   sugar

¼ teaspoon cayenne pepper
1 cup coarsely chopped pecans

In a large saucepan, combine all the ingredients except the pecans; bring to a rolling boil over medium-high heat, stirring constantly. Continue boiling for 8 to 10 minutes, or until the syrup reaches the hard-crack stage (see Note), stirring constantly. Stir in the pecans until completely coated. Immediately pour the brittle onto a large rimmed baking sheet that has been coated with nonstick vegetable spray, spreading with a spatula to make it even, as thick or thin as desired. Be careful: The brittle will be very hot! Allow to cool at room temperature for 30 minutes, then break into pieces and store in an airtight container.

NOTE: The hard-crack stage is reached when a candy thermometer registers between 290°F. and 310°F. To test without a thermometer, remove the pan from the heat and drop ½ teaspoon of the syrup into a cup of cold water. It should form brittle threads that remain brittle when removed from the water.

PECAN PRALINES

ABOUT 3 DOZEN

Looking for a different housewarming gift or stocking stuffer? Try homemade candy! They'll love you for your thoughtfulness . . . and for the yummy goodies!

2 cups pecan halves
2 cups sugar
¾ cup milk

½ teaspoon baking soda
1 tablespoon butter
1½ teaspoons vanilla extract

Line 2 large rimmed baking sheets with waxed paper. Place the pecans, in clusters of 3, about 2 inches apart on the waxed paper. In a medium-sized saucepan, combine the sugar, milk, and baking soda over medium heat. Cook for 18 to 20 minutes, stirring frequently, until the mixture reaches the soft ball stage (see Note). Remove from the heat and stir in the butter and vanilla. Continue stirring for 3 to 5 more minutes, or until the syrup is smooth and creamy and has thickened. Spoon a heaping tablespoon of the syrup mixture over each cluster of pecans. Allow to cool for 1 to 2 hours, then peel from the waxed paper and serve, or place in an airtight container until ready to serve.

NOTE: The soft ball stage is reached when a candy thermometer registers between 234°F. and 240°F. To test without a thermometer, remove the pan from the heat and drop ½ teaspoon of the syrup into a cup of cold water. Remove the cooled syrup from the water and work it with your fingers to form a soft ball. If the ball flattens between your fingers, the syrup has reached the soft ball stage.

INDEX

INDEX

INDEX

INDEX

INDEX

INDEX

INDEX

INDEX

A

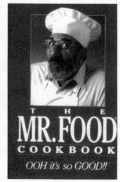

B

C

D

E

F

G

H

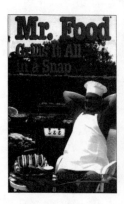

I

J

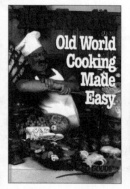

K

L

Mr. Food®'s Library Gives You More Ways to Say...
"OOH IT'S SO GOOD!!®"
WILLIAM MORROW

M

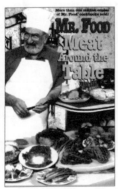

N

O

P

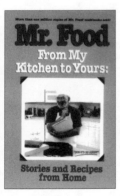

Q

R

S

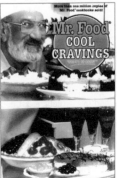

T

Mr. Food ®

Can Help You Be A Kitchen Hero!

Let **Mr. Food** ® make your life easier with
Quick, No-Fuss Recipes and Helpful Kitchen Tips for

Family Dinners • Soups and Salads • Potluck Dishes • Barbecues • Special Brunches • Unbelievable Desserts

. . . and that's just the beginning!

Complete your **Mr. Food** ® cookbook library today.
It's so simple to share in all the *"OOH IT'S SO GOOD!!®"*

✂ -

TITLE	PRICE	QUANTITY	
A. **Mr. Food** ® Cooks Like Mama	@ $12.95 each	x _____	= $_____
B. The **Mr. Food** ® Cookbook, *OOH IT'S SO GOOD!!*®	@ $12.95 each	x _____	= $_____
C. **Mr. Food** ® Cooks Chicken	@ $ 9.95 each	x _____	= $_____
D. **Mr. Food** ® Cooks Pasta	@ $ 9.95 each	x _____	= $_____
E. **Mr. Food** ® Makes Dessert	@ $ 9.95 each	x _____	= $_____
F. **Mr. Food** ® Cooks Real American	@ $14.95 each	x _____	= $_____
G. **Mr. Food** ®'s Favorite Cookies	@ $11.95 each	x _____	= $_____
H. **Mr. Food** ®'s Quick and Easy Side Dishes	@ $11.95 each	x _____	= $_____
I. **Mr. Food** ® Grills It All in a Snap	@ $11.95 each	x _____	= $_____
J. **Mr. Food** ®'s Fun Kitchen Tips and Shortcuts (and Recipes, Too!)	@ $11.95 each	x _____	= $_____
K. **Mr. Food** ®'s Old World Cooking Made Easy	@ $14.95 each	x _____	= $_____
L. "Help, **Mr. Food** ®! Company's Coming!"	@ $14.95 each	x _____	= $_____
M. **Mr. Food** ® Pizza 1-2-3	@ $12.00 each	x _____	= $_____
N. **Mr. Food** ® Meat Around the Table	@ $12.00 each	x _____	= $_____
O. **Mr. Food** ® Simply Chocolate	@ $12.00 each	x _____	= $_____
P. **Mr. Food** ® A Little Lighter	@ $14.95 each	x _____	= $_____
Q. **Mr. Food** ® From My Kitchen to Yours: Stories and Recipes from Home	@ $14.95 each	x _____	= $_____
R. **Mr. Food** ® Easy Tex-Mex	@ $11.95 each	x _____	= $_____
S. **Mr. Food** ® One Pot, One Meal	@ $11.95 each	x _____	= $_____
T. **Mr. Food** ® Cool Cravings	@ $11.95 each	x _____	= $_____

Send payment to:
Mr. Food ®
P.O. Box 9227
Coral Springs, FL 33075-9227

Name _____

Street _____ Apt._____

City _____ State_____ Zip_____

Method of Payment: ☐ Check or Money Order Enclosed

☐ Credit Card: ☐ Visa ☐ MasterCard Expiration Date _____

Signature _____

Book Total $_____

+$2.95 Postage & Handling First Copy *AND* $1 Ea. Add'l. Copy (Canadian Orders Add Add'l. $2.00 *Per Copy*) $_____

Subtotal $_____
Less $1.00 per book if ordering 3 or more books with this order $ –

Add Applicable Sales Tax (FL Residents Only) $_____

Total in U.S. Funds $_____

Account #: ☐ ☐ ☐ ☐ ☐ ☐ ☐ ☐ ☐ ☐ ☐ ☐ ☐ ☐ ☐ ☐

Please allow 4 to 6 weeks for delivery.

BKR